Key to Bird List Symbols

A   Abundantly encountered   Seen on 75–100% of the trips there

C   Commonly encountered   Seen on 50–75% of the trips there

O   Occasionally encountered   Seen on 25–50% of the trips there

R   Rarely encountered   Seen on 1–25% of the trips there

X   Accidental   A unique sighting; needs further explanation

Finding the Birds in Western Mexico

Finding the Birds in Western Mexico

A Guide to the States of Sonora,
Sinaloa, and Nayarit

PETER ALDEN

Color plates by
JOHN O'NEILL

THE UNIVERSITY OF ARIZONA PRESS
Tucson, Arizona

About the Author . . .

PETER ALDEN began bird watching at the age of six in his home town of Concord, Massachusetts. By the time he was sixteen he had watched birds throughout New England, eastern Canada, Texas, and Arizona.

He spent most of his vacations in jungles and on beaches in western Mexico with only a knapsack, binoculars, and a meticulous sight record book. He received a B.A. in geography from the University of Arizona, and during his college years he served as vice president of the Tucson Audubon Society.

Mr. Alden first began guiding bird watching tours in Mexico when the annual convention of the National Audubon Society was held in Tucson in 1964. The popularity of these trips led him to become a partner in a travel agency, which conducts bird-watching trips into Mexico and Latin America. He also conducts bird-watching and natural history tours in various parts of the Old World with the Massachusetts Audubon Society.

Although Mexico has been Mr. Alden's major interest, he has also watched birds in most states of the U.S., Central America, the West Indies, Europe, India, Nepal, Thailand, Malaysia, New Guinea, Australia, New Zealand, and the islands of the South Pacific.

THE UNIVERSITY OF ARIZONA PRESS

In memory of my Mother
Evelyn Engbörg Alden

To the Reader . . .

FOR YEARS the absence of good highways and transportation facilities has kept western Mexico mysterious, isolated, and almost unknown to amateur bird watchers. Bird watching material quite understandably has focused upon the eastern part of the country where for a long time roads and accommodations have been more than adequate, and an impressive number of bird species can be seen.

Travel in the west part of Mexico is no longer difficult, however. A good through railroad serves the area, and recently-completed Highway 15 winds all the way down to Mexico City. Modern bridges now cross rivers which used to be forded by slow, unpunctual ferries. Paved roads branch off Route 15 to such excellent bird watching areas as Alamos, Charay, El Palmito and San Blas. In most places, modern accommodations have grown up along the new thoroughfares, and Guaymas, Mazatlán, and San Blas offer exciting resort facilities.

A growing number of bird watchers, especially from the western parts of the United States, are becoming aware of the new travel conditions in western Mexico. Attracted by the many excellent localities where a great number of unusual endemic and exotic birds can be seen with ease, many of them already have taken bird watching trips through the area, relying on scattered and inadequate literature for guidance.

Their activities have been hampered, of course, by this absence of good material. No field guides had existed for western Mexico, and no book provided color plates of birds common to the area. Good lists of species for specific locales have been few.

This guide is intended to fill these needs. Although it will have many other applications and uses, it has been written and organized primarily to help the amateur bird watcher who is unfamiliar with western Mexico to attain the utmost out of a tour of the Mexican states of Sonora, Sinaloa, and Nayarit. Emphasis has been placed on areas along paved highways and localities easily reached by good roads. A few sidetrips on dirt roads are suggested, but most of these areas do not lie beyond driving distance of good overnight accommodations.

A great part of a bird watching tour is spent en route on the highway. To make this driving time more profitable, good localities beside the roads have been pointed out, and the lists of species include the results of roadside bird watching.

It is hoped that this guide will succeed in making your bird watching trip enjoyable and profitable. Because of the previous isolation of western Mexico, bird records and species lists are still far from adequate. Even professional ornithologists have missed species present in several areas, and misidentifications are often made. The records you keep will be valuable in the revision of present species lists. A word to me in care of the University of Arizona Press concerning any deviations or additions you discover on your trip will be appreciated. Good bird watching!

Acknowledgments

Many individuals have joined me in giving their time and talents to the creation of this work. Foremost is John O'Neill whose fine colored plates greatly increase the value of this book. John is currently dividing his time between ornithological research in the Amazon basin of Peru and graduate studies at Louisiana State University. Clare Ellinwood of Tucson, a long-time birding companion, has offered much-appreciated support of John's work.

Bill Harrison, of Nogales, Arizona, gathered much of the material contained in the sections covering the Magdalena Valley, Hermosillo, and Kino Bay. Peter Hubbell of New York was instrumental in producing the sections on the Durango Highway of Sinaloa and the coastlands of northern Nayarit. Dr. Stephen Russell, curator of birds at the University of Arizona, was of great assistance in the preparation of the sections on Puerto Peñasco and Alamos, Sonora.

Catherine Noble, of Nogales, Arizona, my partner in Mexico-South Tours, has been of immeasurable help in projecting me into and through this work. Daniel Arias, of Nogales, Sonora, has been a matchless companion through tens of thousands of miles of his native Mexico. Darley Gordon, Gladys Mendoza, Polo Acosto, Roberto Balderrama and Miguel Lanzagorta have extended welcomed hospitality to me in western Mexico, as have many fine residents of Alamos and San Blas.

Mrs. Lou Adams of Chico, California, kindly supported a summer study in Nayarit. Peter Willmann of Concord, Massachusetts, joined me in special investigations of Alamos, the Fuerte Valley, and San Blas. Beth Snyder, Alexander (Sandy) Sprunt, Dennis Carter, John Schaefer, Robert Bates, Dennis Coskren, Richard Cunningham, Arnold Small, Mrs. Dick Anderson, the Robert Witzemans, and Ruth Emery have all given invaluable help in lending me their trip records and have offered sound information and advice.

For their interest and inspiration I would like to thank my father, John C. Alden, the Maurice and Forrest Bebbs, Jim Baird, Frank Becherer, Severyn Dana, the Whitney Eastmans, Katherine Hearne, Randolph Jenks, Mary Belle Keefer, Carl Marvel, Grace Miller, Lillian Shields, Ted Steele, Hal Stein, Charles Wood, the Massachusetts and Tucson Audubon Societies, and the many fine people who have seen the birds of Mexico with me.

My final appreciation is voiced to the University of Arizona Press for its confidence, cooperation, and skill in projecting this book into its published form.

PETER ALDEN

Contents

Bird Lists

Maps

Color Plates

Introduction:
How to Use This Guide

THIS BOOK is focused upon field bird watching. Although it is accurate, it is directed more towards the amateur bird watcher than the professional ornithologist. For more detailed scientific information, look to one of the ornithology references listed in Appendix I of this book.

Most questions related to either road directions or bird watching have been anticipated and answered in the text. The numerous questions you will probably have concerning food, lodging, money exchange, language difficulties, and other tourist matters have not been considered here. Because of constantly expanding facilities and advancing road construction, it is felt that an up-to-date tourist guide can do a far better job of answering this kind of question for you. Choose from several fine ones available. The American Automobile Association's *Guide to Mexico and Central America* is especially recommended. Between your tourist manual and this bird watching guide you should find answers to almost all of your questions and enjoy a smooth and profitable trip.

At this writing the following towns have hotel facilities suitable for tourists. In Sonora: Nogales, Puerto Peñasco, Sonoita, Santa Ana, Hermosillo, Kino Bay, Guaymas, Ciudad Obregón, Navajoa, and Alamos. In

Sinaloa: Los Mochis, Topolobampo, Guaymuchil, Culiacán, and Mazatlán. In Nayarit: San Blas and Tepic. Rent-a-car facilities can be had in Tucson, Hermosillo, Ciudad Obregón, Los Mochis, Culiacán, Mazatlán, and Guadalajara.

Although western Mexico is treated with a general north to south orientation, the travel directions in this guidebook are not intended to be a strict itinerary. Often several alternative routes are given, and all of the areas can be seen as you head north instead of south. Include as many or as few of the suggested localities as you wish, depending on time, money, and interest.

The text material does not concentrate upon identification of species. Instead, two highly useful aids have been provided to this purpose. The first of these is the very fine group of color plates from paintings by John O'Neill. These plates illustrate the majority of Mexican species found in Sonora, Sinaloa, and Nayarit. If you find an unfamiliar bird, a glance at one of these realistic pictures will probably clear up your confusion.

Another important tool for identification is the series of species lists. These lists follow the discussions of each major locality, and by giving some idea of what has been seen there in the past can provide clues for identification of any unfamiliar birds you may see

1

there on your trip. The lists may also be of assistance in planning your itinerary insofar as they can help you determine the localities which are most likely to offer the birds which hold special interest for you.

Birds are listed in the order established in the fifth edition of the American Ornithological Union's *Checklist of North American Birds* (1957).

A clear understanding of the system of symbols in the bird lists is important to their efficient use. First, remember that these symbols are derived from field trip sightings. They indicate the number of times a bird actually has been encountered in each locale. This number may not always correspond with the true abundance of the species in the area.

Take, for example, a mangrove swamp in which you see two Great Black Hawks soaring overhead every time you visit it. On only one trip in ten do you sight a Rufous-necked Wood Rail sulking in the foliage. The swamp probably hosts only one pair of hawks, while more than a dozen pairs of wood rails make their nests in the area. Your records, however, indicate that hawks are abundantly encountered, while wood rails are rarely encountered.

The symbol system used in the lists operates on the same basis. Symbols have been limited to single letters in order to leave room for incidental comments:

A   Abundantly encountered—seen on 75–100% of the trips there
C   Commonly encountered—seen on 50–75% of the trips there
O   Occasionally encountered—seen on 25–50% of the trips there
R   Rarely encountered—seen on 1–25% of the trips there
X   Accidental—a unique sighting which needs further explanation

For some lists, other symbols have been devised to convey special information. These marks are explained in the text preceding the lists. No symbols follow bird lists for locales at which field work has not been extensive enough to allow the compilation of accurate seasonal averages.

An asterisk (*) is used in all the lists to indicate birds which are present in the winter and/or during migration periods but are presumed to breed elsewhere. Some of the birds so marked may be absent for only a period of weeks, while others may only be present during a few months. The meaning of this symbol is thus very flexible, its general implication being merely that the bird it applies to cannot always be seen in the area.

In addition to the symbols, miscellaneous relevant comments follow some listed birds. Many of these are notes on where to look for a bird; others indicate the season in which to watch for a species.

For bird species that are difficult to identify accurately in the field, only the generic names have been listed. These names are followed by the word "species" to indicate that more than one kind may have been seen at that locality. For example, the listing "Raven, species," would indicate that both the Common and White-necked Raven may occur. *"Empidonax,* species," indicates that any one of a large group of small flycatchers may have been spotted. Species of flycatchers in the genus *Myiarchus* are sometimes bracketed to show that field identification has not been accurate enough to permit positive species identification.

The bird lists in this volume may differ from those you see in other sources. This is because the lists printed here have been compiled solely from careful records made by the author, members of his bird watching groups, and other reliable field bird watchers during numerous trips taken in various seasons since 1960. Species collected in western Mexico but not confirmed by recent field work have not been included. Any suspiciously strange identifications have been left out. Thus the lists are fairly conservative, omitting such collected species as King Vulture, Amethyst-throated Hummingbird, Imperial Woodpecker, and Olivaceous Woodcreeper, since these have not been seen recently in any of our accessible bird watching locales. Four species for which there seem to be no Mexican specimen have been reported in the area. These are the

Red-necked Grebe, the Horned Grebe, and the Piping Plover at Puerto Peñasco, and the Arctic Tern between Topolobampo and Isla Farallon. These have likewise been left off the lists.

Use Appendix III, a consecutive four-year Christmas bird count taken at San Blas, Nayarit, to gain information on the trends in bird distribution and population in the many types of habitats included in the more tropical areas of Nayarit.

MAP OF WESTERN MEXICO
States of Sonora, Sinaloa, and Nayarit

(Miles between major points given)

CHAPTER I

The Land and the Birds

THE REGION generally referred to as western Mexico extends from the Arizona border through the Mexican states of Sonora, Sinaloa, and Nayarit, a territory approximately 800 miles in length and some 200 miles in width. An unusual variety of natural habitats gives here a more observable abundance of birds than most other regions in the country.

The Deserts

The northern half of the western Mexican lowlands is dry country, with rainfall generally increasing to the south. In northwest Sonora rainfall is under five inches a year, but the average rises to eight to twelve inches in the Hermosillo-Guaymas area and to fifteen inches at Los Mochis.

Rains occur chiefly in July, August, and September with occasional June and October showers. Thunderstorms are most often of short duration, but are frequently very intense, sometimes causing flash floods. Beware of arroyos, or wash gulleys, which may flow with sudden torrents during these rains. Whether in your car or on foot, stay on high ground during desert storms.

Desert winters are mild with afternoon

Chuck Abbott

Giant saguaro cacti typify "Sonoran Desert" type vegetation. Small sturdy cacti, low trees, and scrubby plants dot the ground.

David A. Henderson

The lowlands of southern Sinaloa are covered with thick thorn forest, characterized by a mixture of thorny trees and cacti.

5

temperatures ranging from the sixties to the eighties, depending on elevation and north-south location. Skies are mostly cloudless, although Sonora does have occasional winter drizzles which cause masses of cactus flowers to bloom in the spring season of good years. Summers are quite warm.

Summer bird watching in desert areas should be confined to early morning and evening hours, and a shade hat should always be worn. A full canteen is standard equipment. As a precaution, you might carry a snake bite kit, although poisonous snakes have never been seen on any of our bird watching trips over a period of seven years.

A unique characteristic of the landscape in these regions is the "Sonoran Desert" type of vegetation. This varies according to region and land formation, but the general mixture of giant cacti, small, sturdy cacti, and short, hardy trees prevails throughout. In the summer, a covering of grass often sprouts in various places on the desert floor.

The massive organ pipe, senita, and cardón cacti often reach a height of twenty feet. The famous saguaro cacti may rise to fifty feet. Woodpeckers excavate nest holes in these giants, which are later tenanted by such species such as Elf Owls, Wied's Crested Flycatchers, and Purple Martins. A great variety of birds use the prongy cactus "arms" as perches.

Among the smaller cactus species, the waist-high staghorn and teddy bear cholla are common. Other varieties of cholla and stout columnar barrel cacti may be taller. Clusters of flat prickly pears may cover wide stretches of ground. Check for Roadrunners, Cactus Wrens, and thrashers in and around these thorny plants.

In almost all areas of the desert, but particularly near the banks of arroyos, short scrubby bushes and trees thrive. Prominent among these plants are the stark ocotillos which provide perches for many small species. Green barked palo verde trees bear bright yellow blossoms in the spring. Fragrant creosote bushes blanket many flat

stretches of the desert. Scrubby mesquite and ironwood trees often appear in stands, varying in height according to the presence or absence of water. Southeast of Hermosillo, the leafy jito, the leafless flowering palo santo, and the dramatically branching palo blanco tree almost replace the creosote bush.

Shady cottonwoods and green grass along the river banks present a haven for birds. Eight large rivers flow through western Mexico.

Along the streams and washes, mesquite, scrub oak, and other low trees cluster. Notice the giant cardón cactus in the foreground.

Along desert rivers such as the Magdalena, Sonora, and Yaqui, vegetation is rich and green. Cottonwoods, acacias, and smoke trees thrive, and thick grass grows abundantly along the banks during all seasons of the year. Chiggers, ticks, and biting insects may be a problem in these areas, especially in the summer. Use a spray repellent, stay on the trails, and avoid standing near ant hills.

South of the Rio Yaqui, the low, open desert gradually changes to thick thorn forest as the average annual rainfall increases. Trees become larger, and shrubbery becomes denser. Tangled masses of thorny plants, many of which have mildly poisonous barbs, make these areas nearly impassable. Do not attempt to penetrate these thick "forests" without a guide. Confine your bird watching to the roadside and well-used trails.

The Tropics

The banks of the rivers of northern Sinaloa are an indication of the transition from semi-arid desert to lush tropical jungle. Huge tropical trees like the guanacastle and higuerra (a banyan-like tree with hanging aerial roots) are found along these rivers, and vines bearing fragrant flowers attract many birds.

In San Blas the corozo palm is the dominant tree in the tropical evergreen forests. Coconut palms, strangler figs, tamarindo and tabachin trees, and numerous other tropical trees and plants grow throughout most of Nayarit. Much of the roadside landscape in southern Sinaloa and Nayarit consists of savanna grasslands dotted with palm trees.

The climate in southern Sinaloa, and coastal Nayarit is much more humid than that of Sonora, and features a longer, heavier rainy season from June through October. The heavy rains often occur at night in violent thunderstorms. The palm trees swinging in the rhythm of the rain are an unforgettable sight. The dry season starts in early winter and progresses through May. In late May much of the grazing land is burned in anticipation of the coming rains.

Coastal and inland swamps in these areas are quite dependent on the flooding of the major rivers. The waters spread over these open plains creating a paradise for waterbirds. The greater the floods are, the better it is for bird-watching in the spring months. Due to a lack of good soil conservation practice some places in the mountains, you can probably look forward to heavy floods for many years to come.

Tropical bird watching entails a few special considerations. First, avoid insects by staying away from the beaches after mid-afternoon, using a spray repellant, walking on the roads and paths, and avoiding brushing against weeds. Second, do not try bird watching during the warmer part of the day. Bird activity is at a minimum during these hours, and the air is hot and humid. In both winter and summer restrict your bird watching to the hours from pre-dawn to ten A.M., with perhaps an evening walk through a jungle area.

In all forested areas, wear green or another dark shade of apparel. White clothing may repel birds. It is a good idea to bring a light cloth or poncho to spread on a comfortable log or rock. If you sit quietly and patiently, tropical birds often become unaware of your presence and will venture quite close to you. Become familiar with the calls of common birds in each area and use these notes to locate specimens in the field.

Jaguars, cougars, boa constrictors, and crocodiles live where they can, usually in areas remote from man. They pose little threat if you stay on main trails. The large iguanas of southern Sinaloa and Nayarit are generally harmless. Poisonous spiders and snakes have never been observed by our groups, but you would do well to always remain alert while hiking in the tropics. Stay out of the paths of leaf-cutter ants.

A good set of binoculars is especially important to bird watching in tropical areas, where many birds are active in the towering trees. Wide-angle binoculars are particularly recommended. A telescope is very useful for waterbirds, and perched hawks. A twenty-power eyepiece is quite sufficient, as higher powers are inefficient because of the "heat waves" that rise from the beaches, fields, and waters in a tropical land.

The thick vegetation on the forest floor hides many birds. The best technique for locating them involves a certain amount of patience. When you find a few birds in the dense undergrowth, do not let them out of sight. Often they are with a loose group or "pocket" of their own kind, and it is likely that they will lead you to other species as well.

Few tropical birds other than the finch family show annual plumage variations. If you see a "little brown bird," it is most likely a winter migrant from the north.

Do learn the calls of the common birds in each area. Knowing these will make different calls stand out sharply, drawing your attention to them.

Tall figs and low banana trees dominate the San Blas "lower jungle." This sort of natural forest habitat lies only a few minutes' walk from town. A number of trails make for good bird watching.

The Mountains

Western Mexico is separated from the rest of the mainland by the spectacular ranges of the Sierra Madre Occidental, usually just under 10,000 feet in height. These mountains rise closer and closer to the coastline as it curves eastward, finally meeting the beach dramatically near San Blas, Nayarit.

West of the Sierra Madre Occidental in Sonora and Sinaloa, lower ranges of rugged, disconnected mountains extend in a north-south direction. In the south of Nayarit, however, the mountains near the sea drain off much precipitation, forming a rain shadow in the interior of the state.

Mountain vegetation depends on many variables. In the desert foothills the cacti and low trees become thicker on the mountain slopes, giving way to scrub oaks and finally pines on the taller peaks. In the more tropical areas, lush jungle growth covers the foothills, gradually becoming tropical deciduous forest and then pine-oak forest as the elevation increases.

The tops of the higher peaks in the north

The thick "upper jungle" on the hills outside San Blas supports towering corozo palms, tall fig trees, gumbolimbos, and lush undergrowth. Bird watching here is an exotic and colorful experience.

remain covered with snow well into spring, feeding the major rivers with icy waters. In the south, mountain snow is an uncommon phenomenon. Temperatures, of course, decrease with increasing elevation, producing ideal climates like that of Tépic.

Throughout the Sierra Madre Occidental, steep barrancas (canyons) cut into the mountains. Until recently they have hindered the development of transportation connections. Now, however, adequate roads allow exciting bird watching trips through a wide variety of changing habitats.

One of the most amazing aggregations of plants in Mexico grows on the mountains of Sinaloa. Here tall pine trees are surrounded by tropical magnolias and orchids. Bird life is similarly mingled.

The Coastal Areas

The western borders of all three states of western Mexico are washed by salt water. North of Mazatlán the coasts meet the Gulf of California; south of this city beaches border the great Pacific Ocean. The salt water habitats greatly expand the list of bird species in western Mexico.

In many places the coasts of Nayarit, Sinaloa, and Sonora (as far north as Tiburon Island) are bounded by dense mangrove

swamps. The vast swamps stretch almost continuously between Guaymas and San Blas. Separated from the salt water by barrier beaches and seasonal lagoons, the mangrove swamps keep transportation routes and agriculture a good distance from the coast.

Trackless swamplands of brackish rivers shaded by tall gnarled mangrove trees cover much of the coastal area from Guaymas to San Blas.

The mangrove swamps are a bird watcher's paradise. Their twisting, brackish rivers, marshes, and scattered ponds host one of the largest concentrations of wintering waterbirds in the western hemisphere, and their tall mangrove trees give refuge to countless additional nesting and migrating species. Unfortunately, many of the swamps are trackless, and the clouds of birds which inhabit them are rarely seen by man. Do not attempt to enter these dense swamps without a local guide and a boat. Most of the species in them can be seen nearer the road, although in less staggering numbers.

The fine bathing beaches of Guaymas, Mazatlán and San Blas offer a variety of shorebirds. Rocks sporting colonies of boobies rise from the sea quite close to both San Blas and Mazatlán. Booby rocks are located at greater distances from Topolobampo (near Los Mochis, Sinaloa) and Guaymas.

Boats may be rented for open sea bird watching, and modern ferry crossings can provide inexpensive bird watching trips. At this writing the system of cross-Gulf ferries has been limited to a run between Mazatlán and La Paz, Baja California, but check for newly scheduled routes on your trip.

Just a short way from the coast at Mazatlán rise white-washed "booby rocks," the home of numerous pelagic species. Boats for birdwatching can be readily rented.

In the fall the coasts of all three western Mexican states may be visited by the hurricanes known as *chubascos* or *cordonazos de San Francisco*. These can be very violent; beware of any ominous weather conditions in the autumn.

In the summer and often during other seasons, southern beaches become infested with ajenes, tiny insects which leave an itching, irritating secretion on the skin. Confine beach activities to morning and midday hours during the summer months.

The Influence of Man

In spite of the fact that western Mexico was relatively isolated from the main current of Mexican development until the beginning of this century, today it is the most advanced and prosperous area in the entire country. Between 1950 and 1960 the population increased by 49 per cent. This growth and prosperity, of course, have brought human disturbance of natural bird habitats.

Irrigation has made the area one of the most important agricultural regions in Mexico. Many arid areas in Sonora and northern Sinaloa have been transformed to fertile fields of wheat, cotton, barley, alfalfa, vegetables, and other cash crops. The lowland forests along the stream beds in these regions are being rapidly replaced by farm fields.

While some irrigation water comes from wells, by far the greater part of it is diverted from the rivers. In general, the lakes formed by irrigation dams have not yet become good bird habitats. The water level fluctuates, retarding the development of marshy vegetation, and there is a lack of shallows which most waterbirds prefer. Some irrigation systems are designed to let a steady

Irrigation has made western Mexico an important agricultural region. Many natural habitats have been destroyed, but a stroll along an irrigation ditch can yield an interesting variety of birds.

current of water follow a river bed down to diversion dams where the water is forced into canals. These rivers host an abundance of birds, perhaps more than before dam construction when the flow fluctuated. The water level in the streambeds and pools below the diversion dams, however, is very erratic, and the vegetation and birdlife in these areas have suffered.

The birds which inhabit the irrigated areas may be quite different from those in the surrounding desert. The flooded fields, weedy canals and marshy banks are attracting increasing numbers of herons, geese, tree-ducks, ducks, and shorebirds. Close observation and study of these changes in birdlife may provide answers to important questions concerning human disturbance of natural ecological systems.

In most of Sinaloa and Nayarit, sugar, sesame, tobacco, winter vegetables, coffee, and bananas are important crops. The first four have brought the usual reduction in good bird habitats, but vast banana plantations and particularly coffee plantations in Nayarit host a good variety of tropical species.

Mining and recently lumbering have wrought changes in the mountain areas. The most relevant to birdlife has been the cutting of many of the great pine forests. This logging has affected the seasonal streams on the west coast and has greatly reduced populations of such birds as the Thick-billed Parrot and Imperial Woodpecker.

Hunters have not yet widely affected west Mexican bird populations, although they may do so in the near future. Dove-hunting and water-fowl-hunting are now advertised in the United States. Some serious overhunting occurred near San Blas during the winter of 1967–68, when hunters reduced many huge flocks of Black-bellied Tree Ducks to a few shy, solitary groups. It is hoped that steps will be taken to control such hunting practices.

CHAPTER II

SONORA

ROUTE 15: NOGALES TO SANTA ANA

As YOU CHECK through customs in the city of Nogales, Sonora, eager to see or hear your first Mexican bird, you will encounter some quite familiar species whose presence at such a time will probably disappoint you. Rock Doves and House Sparrows are everywhere in the city. As you approach the car check station four miles south of the international border, you may see flocks of Starlings and a few White-necked Ravens, hear a Rock Wren, and perhaps glimpse a distant Golden Eagle in flight.

Just outside the Nogales city limits, Highway 15 climbs to a pass from which it heads downward into the farming valley of the Rio Magdalena. At the pass and a few miles south of it the highway travels through an oak grassland of widely spaced emory and Mexican blue oaks (live oaks) with thin grass among them. In this upper part of the Magdalena Valley continue watching for Golden Eagles, Acorn Woodpeckers (in the largest oak trees), and noisy flocks of Mexican Jays, for you will not find these three species in the coastal lowlands ahead. Any raven you see along here should be a White-necked Raven. The utility wires are often lined with wintering Sparrow Hawks, Loggerhead Shrikes and Lark Sparrows.

You are required to show your car permit and visas at a check station thirteen miles south of the border. Eight miles beyond this point lies Cibuta, a small settlement indicated by a highway marker. Look for a tiny church on a hill just to the left (east) of the road. A wide dirt road runs right (west) just across the road from the church. Drive down it about a hundred yards until you cross the railroad tracks and arrive at La Posadita Cantina.

Park and walk down to the river. The banks are lined with rich sycamore-cottonwood forest and considerable undergrowth. Hike downstream one quarter mile then return to your car by way of the path along the railroad tracks. This is the northern breeding limit of the Green Kingfisher, which remains on its breeding grounds throughout the winter.

Black Hawks may be seen in summer along the river one quarter mile north of the cantina. (As a general rule, do not start looking for hawks until after ten in the morning.) During invasion winters Lawrence's Goldfinches can be found in the eucalyptus trees behind the cantina. Look for Bendire's Thrashers in the brush along the path south of it.

If you want to do some hiking, continue down the road to kilometer post 2348 and park on the highway beside the railroad tracks. Follow the foot path over the tracks, through two gates, past an old Mexican adobe country home, and into the forest along the river. Cross the loose barbed wire fence on the right and walk upstream one quarter mile or so. This area hosts many migrating and wintering species and some residents that are rather uncommon elsewhere. Look for Rose-throated Becards nesting in the cottonwoods in the summer. Eastern Bluebirds may be singing in the elderberry shrubs along the stream. Keep an eye out for rare migrant Golden-crowned Kinglets as well as autumn Buff-breasted Flycatchers displaying their bright hues high in the cottonwoods.

* * *

At Imuris you may wish to turn off Highway 15 onto a back-country road which crosses the river at two places and rejoins the highway near Magdalena. From September through June it is easily traveled, but during the heavy summer rainy season the stream level may rise dangerously.

To reach the road turn right (west) off Highway 15 at the bus depot, and continue into downtown Imuris. Bear left (south) at the plaza in downtown Imuris, and take an old dirt road past the hot mineral "baños." There is a ford at the edge of Imuris; the hard rock bottom makes crossing easy, but be certain the water isn't too deep. If this ford can be crossed, the remainder of the road will be easy to travel.

For the first few miles the road goes through arid country where you will see your first organ pipe cactus. Look for the Cactus Wren, Bendire's Thrasher, Verdin, and Black-throated Sparrow. The first village is La Mesa, indicated by the marker on the police station hut. Between here and the village of Terrenate the road travels through irrigated fields and orchards where you might see Ground Doves, Lazuli Buntings (during migration) and Cedar Waxwings (winter and late spring).

At Terrenate bear left (east) to reach the river. Here you will cross a second ford, which has a cement bottom. Across the ford at the railroad tracks is the mill at Pierson (indicated by a railroad sign).

Park in the shade of the cottonwoods near the water. You may wish to take some of the little trails that follow the river. Along the railroad tracks that parallel the stream you will find two dirt roads. A stroll along them may prove very productive.

Green Kingfishers hunt from shrubs at the edge of the water. In the summer, look and listen for Gray Hawks near the tall cottonwoods in which they nest. Crissal and Curve-billed Thrashers move through the brush along the stream. Keep an eye out for warblers in the cottonwood forest, particularly during spring migration. Check especially for MacGillivray's Warblers and Painted Redstarts. In the summer Black-chinned and Broad-billed Hummingbirds can be found in the small, yellow-flowered tobacco trees (*Nicotina glauca*). In the winter these hummingbirds are replaced by Anna's Hummingbirds.

Interesting flycatchers in this area include Eastern Phoebes, which can be found occasionally in the winter in the patches of orchard north of the mill. Beardless Flycatchers breed in Tent Caterpillar-infested willows then move into mesquite for the winter. You might find wintering Hooded and Bullock's Orioles and Summer Tanagers in the orange grove south of the mill. Notice the hundreds of Inca Doves that sit in line atop the mill building.

* * *

If you decide not to take this back-country route and still want to do some bird watching in the valley, you can turn right (west) off Highway 15 at the San Ignacio sign about ten miles south of Imuris. Continue past San Ignacio Mission and bear right at every opportunity until you reach the mill at Pierson. Return to the highway via the same route.

Between Imuris and Magdalena Highway 15 passes through the northern limits of a rich desert forest of palo verde, mesquite, ironwood, saguaro and organ pipe. Watch

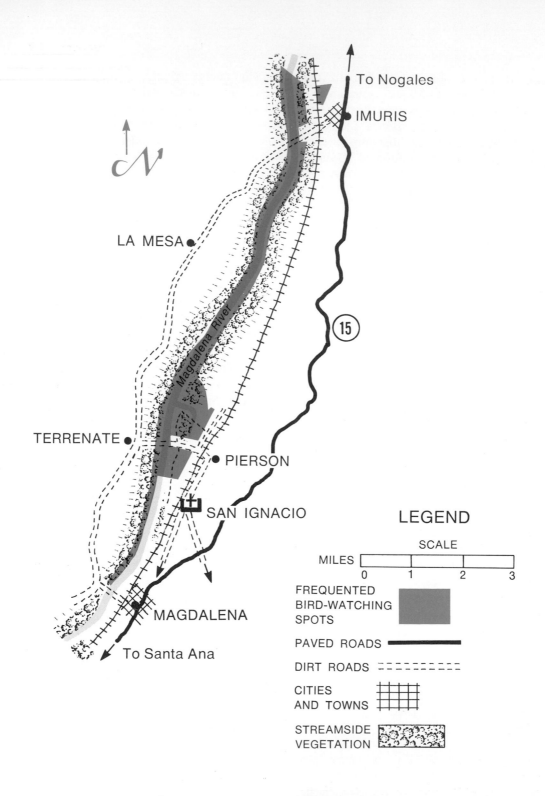

To Nogales

IMURIS

LA MESA

Magdalena River

15

TERRENATE

PIERSON

SAN IGNACIO

LEGEND

SCALE

MILES
0   1   2   3

FREQUENTED
BIRD-WATCHING
SPOTS

PAVED ROADS

DIRT ROADS

CITIES
AND TOWNS

STREAMSIDE
VEGETATION

MAGDALENA

To Santa Ana

MAGDALENA RIVER VALLEY
Imuris to Magdalena, Sonora

here for Caracaras, Gilded Flickers and dozing Great Horned Owls. When you reach Magdalena, check the plaza and outskirts for Bronzed Cowbirds.

Between Magdalena and Santa Ana the highway often follows the river. The banks, however, are highly elevated, preventing easy access to the water from the road. Watch for large soaring birds. Both Black and Turkey Vultures are plentiful at all seasons, and Prairie Falcons have been seen here in winter.

Birds of Nogales and the Magdalena River Valley

Great Blue Heron   C
Common Egret   X   (*January 1966*)
Snowy Egret   O
Green Heron   C
Mallard   O   (*spring*)
Green-winged Teal   O   (*spring*)
Cinnamon Teal   C   (*spring*)
Shoveler   C   (*spring*)
Turkey Vulture   A
Black Vulture   A
Sharp-shinned Hawk   C*
Cooper's Hawk   C*
Red-tailed Hawk   A
Zone-tailed Hawk   O   (*spring*)
Gray Hawk   C   (*summer*)
Black Hawk   O   (*summer*)
Marsh Hawk   C*
Caracara   O
Golden Eagle   C
Prairie Falcon   R*
Pigeon Hawk   R*
Sparrow Hawk   A
Gambel's Quail   A
American Coot   O*
Killdeer   A
Common Snipe   C*
Spotted Sandpiper   C*
Least Sandpiper   C*
Rock Dove   A
White-winged Dove   A
Mourning Dove   A
Ground Dove   A
Inca Dove   A
Yellow-billed Cuckoo   O   (*summer*)
Roadrunner   C
Great Horned Owl   C
Lesser Nighthawk   O   (*summer*)
Vaux's Swift   O   (*migration*)
White-throated Swift   O

Black-chinned Hummingbird   C
  (*summer*)
Anna's Hummingbird   C*
Broad-billed Hummingbird   C   (*summer*)
Belted Kingfisher   C*
Green Kingfisher   A
Red-shafted Flicker   C*
Gilded Flicker   C
Gila Woodpecker   A
Acorn Woodpecker   C   (*oak woodland*)
Yellow-bellied Sapsucker   O*
Ladder-backed Woodpecker   C
Rose-throated Becard   R   (*summer*)
Western Kingbird   A   (*summer*)
Cassin's Kingbird   A   (*summer*)
Wied's Crested Flycatcher   O   (*summer*)
Ash-throated Flycatcher   O   (*summer*)
Olivaceous Flycatcher   O   (*migration*)
Eastern Phoebe   R*
Black Phoebe   A
Say's Phoebe   A
Buff-breasted Flycatcher   R   (*migration*)
Western Wood Pewee   C   (*summer*)
Vermilion Flycatcher   A
Beardless Flycatcher   C
Violet-Green Swallow   O   (*migration*)
Tree Swallow   O   (*migration*)
Rough-winged Swallow   C   (*summer*)
Cliff Swallow   O   (*summer*)
Purple Martin   O   (*migration*)
Mexican Jay   O
White-necked Raven   A
Bridled Titmouse   C
Verdin   A
White-breasted Nuthatch   C*
Brown Creeper   R*
House Wren   C*
Bewick's Wren   A
Cactus Wren   A

Long-billed Marsh Wren   O*
Canyon Wren   C
Rock Wren   C
Mockingbird   C
Bendire's Thrasher   A
Curve-billed Thrasher   A
Crissal Thrasher   C
Robin   C*
Hermit Thrush   C*
Swainson's Thrush   O   (*migration*)
Eastern Bluebird   R   (*summer*)
Blue-Gray Gnatcatcher   C
Golden-crowned Kinglet   X   (*April 1964*)
Ruby-crowned Kinglet   A*
Water Pipit   C*
Cedar Waxwing   O*
Phainopepla   C
Loggerhead Shrike   A
Starling   A   (*Imuris north*)
Bell's Vireo   C*
Solitary Vireo   C   (*migration*)
Warbling Vireo   O   (*migration*)
Orange-crowned Warbler   C*
Lucy's Warbler   A   (*summer*)
Yellow Warbler   C   (*summer*)
Audubon's Warbler   A*
Black-throated Gray Warbler   O*
MacGillivray's Warbler   O   (*migration*)
Yellowthroat   C   (*summer*)
Yellow-breasted Chat   C   (*summer*)
Wilson's Warbler   C   (*migration*)
Painted Redstart   O   (*migration*)
House Sparrow   A
Eastern Meadowlark   R*
Western Meadowlark   C*
Yellow-headed Blackbird   O*
Red-winged Blackbird   C*

Hooded Oriole   O   (*summer*)
Bullock's Oriole   O   (*summer*)
Brewer's Blackbird   C*
Boat-tailed Grackle   A
Brown-headed Cowbird   C
Bronzed Cowbird   C
Western Tanager   C   (*migration*)
Summer Tanager   C   (*summer*)
Cardinal   A
Pyrrhuloxia   A
Black-headed Grosbeak   C   (*migration*)
Blue Grosbeak   C   (*summer*)
Lazuli Bunting   C   (*migration*)
House Finch   A
Pine Siskin   O*
American Goldfinch   R*
Lesser Goldfinch   C
Lawrence's Goldfinch   C*
Green-tailed Towhee   A*
Rufous-sided Towhee   C*
Brown Towhee   A
Lark Bunting   C*
Savannah Sparrow   O*
Vesper Sparrow   C*
Lark Sparrow   C*
Rufous-crowned Sparrow   O   (*on desert hills*)
Black-throated Sparrow   C   (*on desert hills*)
Chipping Sparrow   C*
Brewer's Sparrow   C*
White-crowned Sparrow   A*
White-throated Sparrow   R*
Lincoln's Sparrow   O*
Swamp Sparrow   R*
Song Sparrow   A

PUERTO PEÑASCO

Near the upper reaches of the Gulf of California lies the settlement of Puerto Peñasco (Rocky Point). Only a four hour drive from both Tucson and Phoenix, it can be planned as an interesting day or weekend trip. If you are heading south from Nogales, however, there is little point in taking Mexico Route 2 northwest to Sonoita and Puerto Peñasco; most of the Puerto Peñasco birds are easier to see at other coastal areas.

On Arizona 86 West from Tucson, or U.S. 80 and Arizona 85 from Phoenix, you pass through Organ Pipe Cactus National Monument and arrive at customs. From here paved Mexico Route 8 leads directly to Puerto Peñasco.

HAWKS AND POTOO

Blackish Crane Hawk
Geranospiza nigra

Collared Forest Falcon
Micrastur semitorquatus

Common Potoo
Nyctibius griseus

Laughing Falcon
Herpetotheres cachinnans

Black-collared Hawk
Bursarellus nigricollis

The gateway town to Puerto Peñasco is Sonoita, Sonora, which has resident Starlings. The Sonoita River and dam located two miles east of town are good places to look for birds. Beyond Sonoita you will see typical Sonoran desert vegetation—organ pipe, senita, saguaro, cholla, mesquite, creosote, ironwood, and palo verde—all framed by rocky ridges and peaks. This vegetation becomes sparse as you approach town.

Puerto Peñasco is marked by a bold outcropping of rock near the harbor. It lies on the route of the railroad connecting Baja California with the west coast main line and is the home of a shrimp fleet. Moderate tourist facilities are available.

The Gulf here is much shallower than it is farther south, and its extraordinarily high tidal range may exceed twenty feet. The tide can be quite dangerous as it comes in rapidly.

One good bird watching area is located near a de-salting plant and marine laboratory. This complex can be reached via a well-marked sandy road which goes southeast opposite the Playa Hermosa Hotel. Take this road past an airstrip, a house, and a few tamarisk trees, then turn right (seaward) and cross the railroad tracks on another sandy road marked by a sign. The desalting complex is surrounded by a fence, but you can gain entrance through the watchman. A parking lot lies between the complex and the ocean.

LeConte's Thrashers can be found in the dunes behind the beach. Several species of waterbirds can be seen near the beach and the water. Birds, fish, and interesting invertebrates can be seen in tidal pools during low tide.

The Cholla Bay area, quite popular with bird watchers, is reached on a seven mile dirt road which branches off Mexico 8 about a mile northwest of town. The road is flanked by sand; avoid pulling off of it until you reach one of the parking places.

The Cholla Bay estuary is best for bird watching at high tide, for during low tide birds are scattered over miles of mudflats. Look for shorebirds, gulls and terns at the water's edge. You may glimpse a few passerines behind the beach.

Pelican Point can be reached by driving through the settlement of Cholla Bay, past the camping area, and onto the tip of the point. Most cars make it; if you are in doubt about yours, park at the camping area and walk out to the point. At most times you can see boobies, gulls, terns, and other species of shorebirds.

Norse Beach, behind the Cholla Bay settlement, is another good spot for waterbirds. Surfbirds and Black Turnstones can be found on the rocks here in season. Look over the ocean for loons, grebes, cormorants and boobies.

Birds of Puerto Peñasco

Note: Many of the birds listed here are not followed by abundance symbols because field work has been restricted to several winter months, making the annual status of many species unclear. Puerto Peñasco has very restricted non-coastal habitats, and it is difficult to judge the frequency of migrant landbirds.

Common Loon R (*migration*)	Brown Pelican A
Arctic Loon O (*migration*)	Blue-footed Booby R
Eared Grebe C (*migration*)	Brown Booby C
Western Grebe R*	Double-crested Cormorant R
Fulmar X (*March 1968*)	Brandt's Cormorant R*
Red-billed Tropicbird R	Magnificent Frigatebird C
White Pelican	Great Blue Heron C

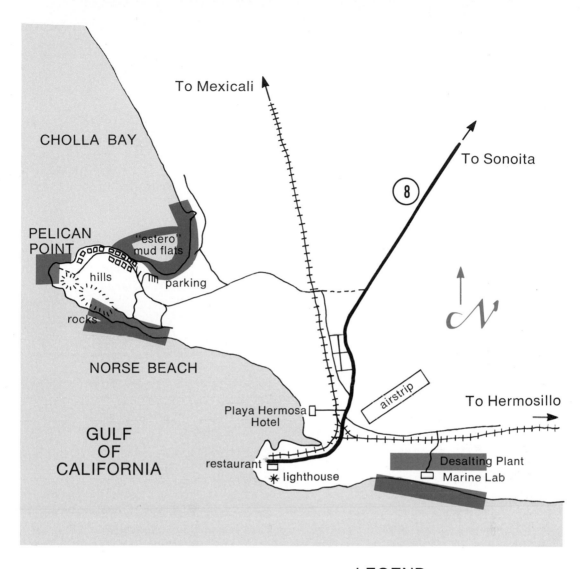

To Mexicali

CHOLLA BAY

PELICAN
POINT

"estero"
mud flats

hills

parking

rocks

NORSE BEACH

GULF
OF
CALIFORNIA

Playa Hermosa
Hotel

restaurant

✱ lighthouse

8

To Sonoita

N

airstrip

To Hermosillo

Desalting Plant
Marine Lab

LEGEND

SCALE

MILES

0   ½   1

FREQUENTED
BIRD-WATCHING
SPOTS

PAVED ROAD ▬▬▬▬▬

SANDY ROAD ─────

PUERTO PEÑASCO, SONORA

Green Heron
Little Blue Heron
Reddish Egret
Snowy Egret   O
Louisiana Heron   O
Mallard
Gadwall
Pintail
Green-winged Teal
American Widgeon
Shoveler
Lesser Scaup
Surf Scoter
Common Merganser   R*
Red-breasted Merganser   A*
Turkey Vulture   A
Black Vulture   R   (*December records*)
Sharp-shinned Hawk
Cooper's Hawk
Red-tailed Hawk   C
Ferruginous Hawk   R*
Osprey   A
Prairie Falcon   (*Route 8 in winter*)
Sparrow Hawk   A
Gambel's Quail   O   (*dunes*)
Sora
American Coot
American Oystercatcher
Semipalmated Plover   A   (*migration*)
Snowy Plover   C
Wilson's Plover   O
Killdeer
Mountain Plover   R*
Black-bellied Plover   A*
Surfbird   O*
Ruddy Turnstone   C*
Black Turnstone   O*
Long-billed Curlew   A*
Whimbrel   O*
Spotted Sandpiper   O*
Wandering Tattler   O*
Willet   A*
Greater Yellowlegs   C*
Lesser Yellowlegs   O*
Knot   R   (*migration*)
Pectoral Sandpiper   R   (*migration*)
Baird's Sandpiper   R   (*migration*)
Least Sandpiper   C*

Dunlin   C   (*migration*)
Dowitcher, species   C*
Western Sandpiper   A*
Marbled Godwit   C*
Sanderling   A*
American Avocet   C*
Wilson's Phalarope
Northern Phalarope   C   (*migration*)
Glaucous-winged Gull   R*
Western Gull   A
Herring Gull   C*
California Gull   O*
Ring-billed Gull   C*
Laughing Gull   R   (*autumn*)
Bonaparte's Gull   C   (*migration*)
Heermann's Gull   A
Forster's Tern   A*
Common Tern   C   (*migration*)
Least Tern   (*summer*)
Royal Tern   A
Elegant Tern   A
Caspian Tern   A
Black Tern   R   (*migration*)
Black Skimmer
White-winged Dove   O   (*summer*)
Mourning Dove   C
Burrowing Owl   R
Long-eared Owl   X   (*October 1964*)
Short-eared Owl   X   (*October 1964*)
Black-chinned Hummingbird   O
Costa's Hummingbird   O
Anna's Hummingbird   O*
Belted Kingfisher
Gila Woodpecker
Ladder-backed Woodpecker
Cassin's Kingbird
Western Kingbird
Ash-throated Flycatcher
Say's Phoebe
Vermilion Flycatcher   R
Tree Swallow   (*October records*)
Barn Swallow   (*October records*)
Raven, species
Verdin   C
Cactus Wren
Rock Wren   R*
Mockingbird   A
Curve-billed Thrasher   O

Le Conte's Thrasher   C
Sage Thrasher   R*
Mountain Bluebird   R
Ruby-crowned Kinglet   A*
Water Pipit
Phainopepla   C   (*Route 8*)
Loggerhead Shrike   O
Starling   R
Orange-crowned Warbler
Yellow Warbler
Audubon's Warbler
Black-throated Gray Warbler
MacGillivray's Warbler
Wilson's Warbler
House Sparrow   A

Brewer's Blackbird
Brown-headed Cowbird
Painted Bunting
House Finch   C
Savannah Sparrow   A   (*A Mexican sub-species known as Large-billed Sparrow breeds here.*)
Vesper Sparrow
Lark Sparrow
Sage Sparrow   R*
Chipping Sparrow
Brewer's Sparrow   O*
White-crowned Sparrow
Golden-crowned Sparrow   R*
Lincoln's Sparrow

ROUTE 15: SANTA ANA TO HERMOSILLO

AS YOU TRAVEL through the rich desert vegetation between Santa Ana and Hermosillo, you may find groups of colorful Caracaras gathered by the roadside, eating animals killed by passing cars. At any spot where grass is growing along a wide desert wash, look for resident Rufous-winged Sparrows which should be singing from March through July. Vaux's Swifts have been seen here in migration, flying low over the vegetation while searching for insects. House Finches are common and noisy in the desert. You may see Roadrunners dashing across the highway ahead of your car.

On the outskirts of Hermosillo to the left of the highway is a large reservoir which stores water from the Sonora River for irrigation of tracts coastward from the city. The water level fluctuates greatly behind the dam and is usually highest in autumn.

A few miles beyond the reservoir, Route 15 runs into a major rotary intersection which has a statue of Father Kino in its center. If you stay on Route 15, you will go through the center of beautiful, modern Hermosillo and continue south towards Guaymas. Be sure to stop to look for Bronzed Cowbirds and Scarlet-headed Orioles in the beautifully landscaped plaza across from the cathedral.

The right (west) branch of the intersection is a paved bypass of the city which joins Sonora Route 16 to Kino Bay, a sidetrip discussed in the next section. By going three-quarters of the way around the rotary and turning on Calle Las Virgenes, you can take in the Hermosillo dam and reservoir. Beyond the reservoir, this road rejoins Route 15 South to Guaymas.

About a mile from the rotary, Calle Las Virgenes passes through a parkland below the dam. The small trees, grassy areas, and marshy channels attract Song Sparrows. Land birds gather here during migration in very early March. From March through July Bell's Vireos can be heard singing in the shrubs.

You will probably want to continue on to the southern edge of the dam where you can scan the entire reservoir for water birds. With a good telescope you should be able to see cormorants, herons, egrets, ibis, ducks, and shorebirds, except during the very lowest water levels.

Birds Between Santa Ana and Hermosillo, Including Hermosillo

Pied-billed Grebe   C*
White Pelican   O*
Double-crested Cormorant   O*
Olivaceous Cormorant   O
Great Blue Heron   C
Green Heron   C
Little Blue Heron   R
Common Egret   O
Snowy Egret   C
Louisiana Heron   O   (*autumn*)
Wood Ibis   O   (*autumn*)
White-faced Ibis   O
Roseate Spoonbill   X   (*October 1967*)
Black-bellied Tree Duck   O
Mallard   C*
Gadwall   C*
Pintail   C*
Green-winged Teal   C*
Blue-winged Teal   O*
Cinnamon Teal   C*
American Widgeon   C*
Shoveler   C*
Ring-necked Duck   C*
Canvasback   O*
Lesser Scaup   C*
Bufflehead   O*
Ruddy Duck   C*
Turkey Vulture   A
Black Vulture   A
Cooper's Hawk   O*
Red-tailed Hawk   A
Swainson's Hawk   C   (*migration*)
Harris' Hawk   O
Marsh Hawk   O*
Caracara   A
Prairie Falcon   R*
Sparrow Hawk   C
Gambel's Quail   C
American Coot   A*
Killdeer   A
Spotted Sandpiper   C*
Willet   O*
Greater Yellowlegs   C   (*migration*)
Lesser Yellowlegs   C   (*migration*)
Pectoral Sandpiper   O   (*migration*)

Least Sandpiper   C*
Long-billed Dowitcher   C*
Western Sandpiper   O*
American Avocet   O*
Black-necked Stilt   O
Wilson's Phalarope   C   (*migration*)
Western Gull   O*
Ring-billed Gull   C*
Franklin's Gull   O   (*migration*)
Common Tern   R   (*autumn*)
Black Tern   O   (*migration*)
Rock Dove   A
White-winged Dove   A
Mourning Dove   A
Ground Dove   A
Inca Dove   A
Roadrunner   C
Great Horned Owl   O
Lesser Nighthawk   C   (*summer*)
Vaux's Swift   O   (*migration*)
Broad-billed Hummingbird   O
Belted Kingfisher   C
Gilded Flicker   C
Gila Woodpecker   A
Ladder-backed Woodpecker   C
Western Kingbird   A   (*migration*)
Cassin's Kingbird   A
Wied's Crested Flycatcher   O   (*summer*)
Ash-throated Flycatcher   C
Black Phoebe   A
Say's Phoebe   A
Traill's Flycatcher   O
Vermilion Flycatcher   A
Violet-Green Swallow   O   (*migration*)
Rough-winged Swallow   C
Barn Swallow   C   (*migration*)
Raven, species   C
Verdin   A
Bewick's Wren   C*
Cactus Wren   C
Long-billed Marsh Wren   C*
Canyon Wren   C
Rock Wren   C
Mockingbird   C
Phainopepla   O

Loggerhead Shrike   A
Starling   O
Bell's Vireo   C
Audubon's Warbler   C*
Yellowthroat   C
Wilson's Warbler   C*
House Sparrow   A
Western Meadowlark   C
Yellow-headed Blackbird   C*
Red-winged Blackbird   A
Bullock's Oriole   O
Scarlet-headed Oriole   R
Brewer's Blackbird   C*
Boat-tailed Grackle   A

Brown-headed Cowbird   C
Bronzed Cowbird   C
Cardinal   C
Pyrrhuloxia   O
Lazuli Bunting   O*
House Finch   A
Brown Towhee   C
Lark Bunting   C*
Lark Sparrow   C
Rufous-winged Sparrow   O
Black-throated Sparrow   C
White-crowned Sparrow   A*
Lincoln's Sparrow   C*
Song Sparrow   A

SIDETRIP: HERMOSILLO TO KINO BAY

KINO BAY on the Gulf of California is visited frequently by bird watchers on weekend trips from Arizona. If your particular interest is waterbirds or if you would like to see some Seri Indians (a relatively primitive group which inhabits the coast north of the Bay) you may want to make it a part of your trip.

Kino Bay lies seventy miles west of Hermosillo on paved Sonora Route 16. Route 16 starts a block north of the University of Sonora in Hermosillo and is well marked. It can be reached even more easily by taking the bypass route which branches west at the major rotary intersection on the northern outskirts of the city.

The road travels through mesquite grasslands and cultivated fields until it passes through an isolated group of hills twenty-two miles west of Hermosillo. You might want to stop and walk up one of these gentle hillsides. Their desert slopes are still the homes of such birds as the Broad-billed Hummingbird, Canyon Wren, and Black-throated Sparrow, whose former habitats have been changed by cultivation.

Just beyond the hills a paved road turns left (south) towards Guaymas to join Route 15. This is a good shortcut to use on your return trip. A network of dirt roads also branch off Route 16, traveling through vast irrigated stands of cotton, wheat, and orange trees. You may find migrant water birds in the flooded fields. Before you reach the Gulf, you will pass through several miles of giant cactus forest.

There are essentially two towns on Kino Bay. As the waters of the Gulf become visible you will notice several well-traveled dirt roads leading left (south) to Old Kino, the original town, now only a group of small adobes.

The modern buildings of New Kino line the paved road which travels north for several miles along the coast. Fine beach houses, palm trees, sidewalks, and a new plaza indicate prosperity. Restaurants and overnight facilities are located beyond the plaza.

The New Kino road comes to an abrupt end at a tall hill near the shoreline. The restaurant Caverna del Seri at the foot of the hill is an excellent point from which to scan for loons, pelicans, boobies, cormorants, gulls and terns.

One good bird watching area at Kino Bay lies north of the Caverna del Seri. A dirt road leads right (east) inland through lush desert vegetation. The washes or gulleys which lead to the Gulf may host Black-tailed Gnatcatchers, Rock Wrens, Pyrrhuloxia, and wintering Green-tailed Towhees. Shortly after passing a small airstrip on your right, turn left (seaward) on either of two dirt spurs. These roads both lead to a good vantage point for scanning for deep water birds.

A much better group of vantage points can be reached by passing these spurs and following the main dirt road as it winds right, and soon turns back to the sea. (Total distance from the paved New Kino Road is a mile and a half.) As you near the water, three spurs lead to prominent bluffs. The two on the left are best for scanning.

You may want to walk down a wash to the beach to inspect the tidal rocks for rock shorebirds and invertebrates. These rocks host wintering Surfbirds and Black Turnstones. They are good spots from which to scan the ocean.

A different type of bird watching area lies along the good dirt road leading south from the town of Old Kino. It passes behind the dunes, then skirts a shallow estuary lined with mangrove trees. Mangrove Warblers (a red-headed color phase of the Yellow Warbler) sing high in the branches in the summer.

Stop along the road when you find a good vantage point to scan the mudflats for waders. Among the more exciting birds you may find are Reddish Egrets, Wood Ibis, White Ibis, Roseate Spoonbills, American Oystercatchers, Snowy Plovers, Wilson's Plovers, and Long-billed Curlews. Ospreys and various terns can be seen overhead.

The road ends at a dock and a charter fishing facility. This area is accessible at all times except during unusually high tides. Watch for soft sandy patches near the end of the road.

Birds of Kino Bay

Common Loon   A*
Arctic Loon   O*
Eared Grebe   A*
Western Grebe   O*
White Pelican   O*
Brown Pelican   A
Blue-footed Booby   A
Brown Booby   A
Double-crested Cormorant   A
Magnificent Frigatebird   A   (*summer*)
Great Blue Heron   A
Common Egret   A
Snowy Egret   A
Reddish Egret   O
Louisiana Heron   O
Little Blue Heron   O
Green Heron   A*
Wood Ibis   O
White Ibis   O
Roseate Spoonbill   O
Black-bellied Tree Duck   (*irrigated districts*)
Lesser Scaup   (*irrigated districts*)
Bufflehead   (*irrigated districts*)
Common Merganser   A*

Red-breasted Merganser   C*
Turkey Vulture   A
Black Vulture   A
Red-tailed Hawk   A
Harris' Hawk   O*
Marsh Hawk   R*
Osprey   A
Sparrow Hawk   C
Gambel's Quail   A
American Oystercatcher   O
Semipalmated Plover   O*
Snowy Plover   C
Wilson's Plover   O
Killdeer   A
Mountain Plover   R*
Black-bellied Plover   O*
Surfbird   C*
Black Turnstone   C*
Long-billed Curlew   A*
Whimbrel   C*
Spotted Sandpiper   A*
Solitary Sandpiper   C   (*migration*)
Willet   A*
Greater Yellowlegs   C*
Lesser Yellowlegs   C*

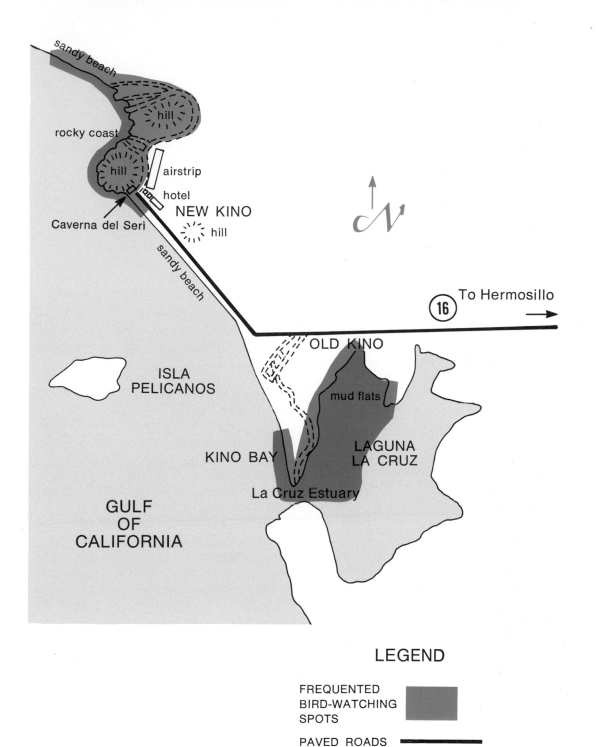

sandy beach

rocky coast

hill

hill

airstrip

hotel

Caverna del Seri

NEW KINO

hill

sandy beach

To Hermosillo

16

ISLA
PELICANOS

OLD KINO

mud flats

KINO BAY

LAGUNA
LA CRUZ

La Cruz Estuary

GULF
OF
CALIFORNIA

LEGEND

FREQUENTED
BIRD-WATCHING
SPOTS

PAVED ROADS

DIRT ROADS

KINO BAY, SONORA

Least Sandpiper   A*
Dunlin   O*
Long-billed Dowitcher   A*
Western Sandpiper   C*
Marbled Godwit   C*
Sanderling   C*
American Avocet   C*
Black-necked Stilt   C
Western Gull   A
Herring Gull   O*
California Gull   C*
Ring-billed Gull   A*
Bonaparte's Gull   O*
Heermann's Gull   A
Forster's Tern   O*
Royal Tern   C
Elegant Tern   O
Caspian Tern   C
White-winged Dove   A
Mourning Dove   A
Ground Dove   A
Inca Dove   A
Roadrunner   C
Lesser Nighthawk   C   (*summer*)
Broad-billed Hummingbird   C
Gilded Flicker   A
Gila Woodpecker   A
Ladder-backed Woodpecker   C
Ash-throated Flycatcher   C*
Black Phoebe   C
Say's Phoebe   A
Vermilion Flycatcher   O
Violet-Green Swallow   C   (*migration*)
Rough-winged Swallow   O
Barn Swallow   O   (*summer*)
Raven, species   C

Verdin   A
Bewick's Wren   A*
Cactus Wren   A
Canyon Wren   C
Rock Wren   C
Mockingbird   A
Bendire's Thrasher   C
Curve-billed Thrasher   C
Black-tailed Gnatcatcher   O
Phainopepla   C
Loggerhead Shrike   A
Yellow Warbler   C
Audubon's Warbler   C*
House Sparrow   A
Western Meadowlark   C*
Yellow-headed Blackbird   C*   (*irrigated districts*)
Red-winged Blackbird   A*   (*irrigated districts*)
Brewer's Blackbird   A*   (*irrigated districts*)
Boat-tailed Grackle   A
Brown-headed Cowbird   C
Cardinal   A   (*dunes*)
Varied Bunting   O   (*irrigated districts*)
House Finch   A
Green-tailed Towhee   C*
Brown Towhee   C
Lark Bunting   C*
Savannah Sparrow   C   (*summer*)
Lark Sparrow   C*
Black-throated Sparrow   C
White-crowned Sparrow   A
Lincoln's Sparrow   O*   (*irrigated districts*)

ROUTE 15: HERMOSILLO TO GUAYMAS

THIS TRIP through mesquite grassland desert takes under two hours. Birdlife is much the same as that south of Santa Ana. White-tailed Hawks vie with the Red-tails, Harris' Hawks, and Swainson's Hawks for the tops of cacti and telephone poles. Caracaras should be conspicuous. In winter try to spot Sage Thrashers among the many sparrows.

Just south of kilometer post 2027 you will find a depression which fills with water after the rains, attracting such birds as Eared Grebes, Pied-billed Grebes, Green-winged Teals, Shovelers, Redheads, Lesser Scaups, Ruddy Ducks, Caracaras, Black Phoebes, Vermilion Flycatchers, Lark Buntings, numerous sparrows and some shorebirds. Just beyond the post a paved road branches off to the right (west) to Kino Bay, then connects with Route 16 from Hermosillo.

As you approach Guaymas, signs point west to San Carlos Bay, a relatively new development with full facilities, including a new hotel. Here you will see some oceanside and desert species. Buff-collared Nightjars inhabit a canyon lined with wild palms.

Clerks at most of the hotels and motels can direct you to this unusual barranca.

If you continue on Route 15, you will bypass Guaymas and head south to Navojoa. About a mile to the north of town, a wide avenue branches off of Route 15 and leads into the heart of the Guaymas business district.

GUAYMAS

GUAYMAS, the major seaport north of Mazatlán, occupies a deep mountain-rimmed valley washed by the Gulf of California. The desert vegetation continues to the edge of the sea, producing a stark kind of beauty. Although there are several modestly priced hotels downtown, most facilities are located along the road north of town and along the beach at Bacochibampo Bay.

The main business street of Guaymas ends at a small park on the waterfront. Turn right onto the major boulevard which branches west near the park and continue along the edge of the harbor for several miles. In addition to striking views of the ocean and a beautiful palm-lined beach, many species of birds can be seen here. A great number of the species listed for Tular Lagoon will be seen along this road, although in lesser numbers. If your visit is in April or May, watch carefully for Kiskadee Flycatchers and Mangrove Swallows. In the winter the deep harbor waters support rafts of Eared Grebe, Lesser Scaup, and Bufflehead. A number of Arctic Loons can usually be sighted on the water. The shrimp boats attract large numbers of gulls.

Boats can be chartered from your hotel or rented at the dock. Several booby islands are located just offshore, conspicuous by their lack of vegetation and bright coats of whitewash. On a late-March boat trip into the Gulf of California, the following birds, in addition to gulls, were seen:

Eared Grebes—many
Black Petrels—thousands
Least Petrels—thousands
Red-billed Tropicbirds—a few
Blue-footed Boobies—several dozen
Brown Boobies—several dozen
Northern Phalaropes—thousands
Xantus' Murrelets—a few dozen

Bacochibampo Bay, fringed by Miramar beach, is reached by a well-marked road. Turn right (southwest) on the only paved road going seaward on the northern edge of Guaymas. Notice the dirt road that branches right (west) to Tular Lagoon and the fine residential area known as Las Tinajas.

As you approach the beach, two big hotels stand on the left. The grounds around both are heavily planted with palms, bougainvillaea, bananas, and various other trees and flowers. This lush vegetation gives refuge to desert-weary birds and provides a limited habitat for species more common further south. You may have the good fortune to find such tropical specimens as the Violet-crowned Hummingbird, Kiskadee Flycatcher, Mangrove Swallow, Rufous-backed Robin and Scarlet-headed Oriole.

From the hotels you can scan the bay for members of several marine families: loons, grebes, pelicans, boobies, cormorants, frigatebirds, mergansers, shorebirds, gulls, and terns. Behind the Hotel Miramar a dirt road leads back through the desert to a little irrigated oasis which, though private property, is open to bird watchers. Many species such as Allen's Hummingbird can be found here in the winter.

Tular lagoon behind Miramar Beach is gradually being filled in. This operation is destroying one of the best easily accessible waterbird havens in western Mexico. The sections near the hotels already have been filled, but you can still find many birds by going back toward the main highway, turning north, and proceeding along the dirt road towards Las Tinajas. When you arrive at the backwater you will see a marshy area with a thicket to its right. This area has always been full of interesting birds, and many

accidentals have been recorded here. A dirt road to the right (north) takes you to the edge of the thicket and is a good place for a leisurely walk.

After seeing this area, continue on the road beside the lagoon, stopping frequently to observe waterbirds. As you near the sea you will come upon a group of mangroves. These trees offer homes to many roosting herons and egrets, particularly Night Herons. Where the road passes the washed-out bridge which formerly connected the hotels to this area, you will find excellent elevated positions from which to scan for marine birds.

Birds of Guaymas

Common Loon   C*
Arctic Loon   A*
Eared Grebe   A*
Western Grebe   O*
Pied-billed Grebe   R*
Brown Pelican   A
Blue-footed Booby   A   (*over the Gulf*)
Brown Booby   C   (*over the Gulf*)
Double-crested Cormorant   A   (*huge migration concentrations*)
Olivaceous Cormorant   R
Brandt's Cormorant   R*
Magnificent   Frigatebird   A   (*over the Gulf*)
Great Blue Heron   A
Green Heron   O
Little Blue Heron   A
Reddish Egret   C
Common Egret   O
Snowy Egret   A
Louisiana Heron   A
Black-crowned Night Heron   O
Yellow-crowned Night Heron   O
Least Bittern   R   (*December records*)
Wood Ibis   R
White-faced Ibis   R   (*spring records*)
White Ibis   A
Roseate Spoonbill   O   (*summer*)
Mallard   R*
Gadwall   O*

Pintail   C*
Green-winged Teal   C*
Blue-winged Teal   R*
American Widgeon   C*
Shoveler   C*
Redhead   O*
Ring-necked Duck   O*
Canvasback   R*
Lesser Scaup   A*
Common Goldeneye   R*
Bufflehead   A*
Surf Scoter   R*
Ruddy Duck   O*
Red-breasted Merganser   A*
Turkey Vulture   A
Black Vulture   A
Red-tailed Hawk   C
Osprey   C
Caracara   O
Aplomado Falcon   X   (*summer 1966*)
Pigeon Hawk   R*
Sparrow Hawk   C
Gambel's Quail   O
American Coot   O*
American Oystercatcher   O
Semipalmated Plover   C*
Snowy Plover   R
Wilson's Plover   C
Killdeer   A
Black-bellied Plover   O*

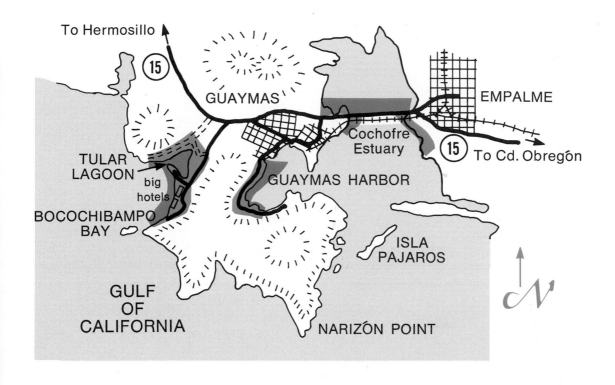

To Hermosillo

(15)

GUAYMAS

EMPALME

Cochofre
Estuary

(15) To Cd. Obregón

TULAR
LAGOON

big
hotels

GUAYMAS HARBOR

BOCOCHIBAMPO
BAY

ISLA
PAJAROS

GULF
OF
CALIFORNIA

NARIZÓN POINT

N

LEGEND

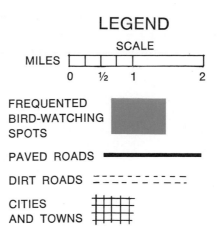

SCALE

MILES

| 0 | ½ | 1 | | 2 |

FREQUENTED
BIRD-WATCHING
SPOTS

PAVED ROADS

DIRT ROADS

CITIES
AND TOWNS

GUAYMAS, SONORA

Ruddy Turnstone   R*
Common Snipe   R*
Long-billed Curlew   A*
Whimbrel   A*
Spotted Sandpiper   A*
Solitary Sandpiper   R   (*migration*)
Willet   A
Greater Yellowlegs   A*
Lesser Yellowlegs   A*
Knot   R*
Least Sandpiper   A*
Dunlin   R*
Dowitcher, species   O*
Western Sandpiper   A*
Marbled Godwit   A*
Sanderling   R*
American Avocet   A*
Black-necked Stilt   R
Northern Phalarope   R*
Western Gull   A
Herring Gull   R*
California Gull   C*
Ring-billed Gull   A*
Laughing Gull   O
Bonaparte's Gull   C*
Heermann's Gull   A
Forster's Tern   A*
Least Tern   A   (*summer*)
Royal Tern   C
Elegant Tern   C
Caspian Tern   A
Black Skimmer   C   (*summer*)
White-winged Dove   A
Mourning Dove   C
Ground Dove   C
Inca Dove   A
Roadrunner   R
Lesser Nighthawk   O
Black-chinned Hummingbird   C
Costa's Hummingbird   C
Allen's Hummingbird   C*
Violet-crowned   Hummingbird   R   (*autumn*)
Broad-billed Hummingbird   A
Belted Kingfisher   A
Red-shafted Flicker   R*
Gilded Flicker   C
Gila Woodpecker   A

Ladder-backed Woodpecker   C
Western Kingbird   O
Cassin's Kingbird   C
Kiskadee Flycatcher   C   (*late spring*)
Ash-throated Flycatcher   O*
Black Phoebe   O
Say's Phoebe   C*
Western Flycatcher   R*
Vermilion Flycatcher   O
Violet-Green   Swallow   O   (*March records*)
Tree Swallow   O   (*migration*)
Mangrove Swallow   O   (*April*)
Rough-winged Swallow   O
Raven, species   A
Verdin   A
House Wren   O*
Cactus Wren   A
Long-billed Marsh Wren   R*
Canyon Wren   O
Rock Wren   A
Mockingbird   A
Bendire's Thrasher   O
Curve-billed Thrasher   A
American Robin   X   (*December, 1967*)
Rufous-backed   Robin   R   (*October and April records*)
Hermit Thrush   O*
Blue-Gray Gnatcatcher   O*
Black-tailed Gnatcatcher   C
Ruby-crowned Kinglet   O*
Phainopepla   O
Loggerhead Shrike   A
Bell's Vireo   C   (*migration*)
Solitary Vireo   O*
Orange-crowned Warbler   A*
Nashville Warbler   O*
Yellow Warbler   O
Audubon's Warbler   C*
Wilson's Warbler   O*
House Sparrow   A
Meadowlark, species   R
Red-winged Blackbird   R
Hooded Oriole   A
Scarlet-headed Oriole   O
Bullock's Oriole   O
Brewer's Blackbird   O*
Boat-tailed Grackle   A

Brown-headed Cowbird   C*
Bronzed Cowbird   C
Cardinal   A
Pyrrhuloxia   A
Blue Grosbeak   R
Lazuli Bunting   R*
Varied Bunting   R
House Finch   A
Lesser Goldfinch   R
Green-tailed Towhee   C*
Brown Towhee   A
Lark Bunting   A*   (*flight winters*)
Savannah Sparrow   R
Vesper Sparrow   O*

Lark Sparrow   A
Rufous-winged Sparrow   C
Black-throated Sparrow   C
Gray-headed Junco   X   (*November, 1963*)
Chipping Sparrow   O*
Clay-colored Sparrow   O*
Brewer's Sparrow   C*
White-crowned Sparrow   A*
White-throated Sparrow   X   (*November 1963*)
Lincoln's Sparrow   O*
Swamp Sparrow   X   (*December 1965*)

ROUTE 15: GUAYMAS TO NAVOJOA, INCLUDING SIDETRIPS

AS YOU HEAD EAST out of Guaymas on Route 15, you will cross a long causeway from which you will see a wide inlet. Check for Reddish Egrets, Magnificent Frigatebirds, and Laughing Gulls. In the winter months you may find Western Grebes, Eared Grebes, White Pelicans, and Red-breasted Mergansers.

When you reach the "Empalme side" of the causeway on the east, park beside the road and make a closer check of the waterbirds on the inlet. Walk across the railroad tracks which parallel the causeway and look out into the Gulf. You may see wintering loons, grebes, and Lesser Scaup. The wide mudflats to your left are usually covered with shorebirds, especially Marbled Godwits and dowitchers. Various herons and egrets (including Louisiana Herons), ducks, plovers, curlews, and Black Skimmers may also be found here.

After leaving Empalme, a railroad town and former bracero center, you will pass through more dry desert landscape with irrigated farms on the left (north) side of the road. The Guaymas N.A.S.A. Tracking Station stands on the north side of the highway. Some ponds just beyond kilometer post 1925 may have various interesting birds. In the summer look for Roseate Spoonbills, Least Grebes, and Purple Martins. Common Gallinules become a familiar roadside bird from this point south. Hawks, Caracaras, Gambel's Quail, Roadrunners, and White-necked Ravens are the larger roadside birds along this route. Harris' Hawks and White-necked Ravens make nests high up on the tall electricity transmission poles along the highway.

As you continue east you will notice a string of tall cottonwood trees far to your right, parallel to the road. These line the banks of the Yaqui River, one of the major rivers of the Sierra Madre watershed. Man has altered the course of the Yaqui, trapping its waters behind Obregón Dam and diverting them into an extensive irrigation system. Only reedy remnant sloughs exist where a year-round river once flowed. As long as the sloughs remain, however, the area is still fine for bird watching. A variety of birds are attracted by the shallow puddles of water, and the rich vegetation on the river banks has not yet noticeably thinned.

Highway 15 will take you through Vicam, the chief town of the once-fierce Yaqui Indians. Harris' Hawks are quite common in this area. If you are in a hurry, continue on Route 15 to Ciudad Obregón. The best bird watching is along the river bed, although it is not easily acessible from the highway. Look for couples of White-fronted Parrots crossing the treetops. This is the approximate northern limit of their habitat.

* * *

A more interesting route to Ciudad Obregón that will take you straight to the river bed is a shortcut on an unnumbered paved road which turns right (south) between kilometer posts 1181 and 1180 about 65 miles beyond Empalme, just after a sluice-like waterfall in the canal that runs along the south side of Highway 15. This route leads to Bacum across the bed of the Yaqui River.

The road will soon take you into the tall forest along the river bed. Park here and slowly stroll along the banks, watching for birds in the tall trees and brushy tracts. Walk upstream and look down on the remnant sloughs, always keeping an eye cocked for the bird activity overhead. Notice especially the very noisy groups of Social Flycatchers high in the treetops.

Birds of the Yaqui River Crossing, Bacum

Bare-throated Tiger Heron   O   (*November and December records*)
Turkey Vulture   A
Black Vulture   A
Gray Hawk   O
Caracara   C
Sparrow Hawk   A
Virginia Rail   R   (*October record*)
Sora   O   (*April records*)
Common Gallinule   R
American Coot   O*
Killdeer   O
White-winged Dove   A
Mourning Dove   A
Ground Dove   A
Inca Dove   A
Barn Owl   R
Violet-crowned Hummingbird   O
Broad-billed Hummingbird   A
Green Kingfisher   O
Gilded Flicker   A
Red-shafted Flicker   O*
Gila Woodpecker   A
Ladder-backed Woodpecker   A
Rose-throated Becard   O   (*A in summer*)
Tropical Kingbird   R
Western Kingbird   C
Cassin's Kingbird   A
Social Flycatcher   A
Kiskadee Flycatcher   O   (*April records*)
Olivaceous Flycatcher   C
Black Phoebe   O

Western Flycatcher   O*
Vermilion Flycatcher   A
Beardless Flycatcher   O
Tree Swallow   O   (*migration*)
Rough-winged Swallow   C
Barn Swallow   O   (*migration*)
White-necked Raven   C
Mexican Crow   R   (*October record*)
House Wren   O*
Cactus Wren   A
Mockingbird   C
Curve-billed Thrasher   O
Hermit Thrush   R*
Blue-Gray Gnatcatcher   C*
Ruby-crowned Kinglet   O*
Black-and-White Warbler   X   (*December 1964*)
Orange-crowned Warbler   C*
Yellow Warbler   C*   (*spring*)
Audubon's Warbler   C*
Black-throated Gray Warbler   O*
MacGillivray's Warbler   O*
Yellowthroat   C
Wilson's Warbler   C*
American Redstart   X   (*December 1964*)
Hooded Oriole   R   (*April records*)
Scarlet-headed Oriole   A
Boat-tailed Grackle   A
Cardinal   A
Pyrrhuloxia   A
House Finch   A
Lesser Goldfinch   C

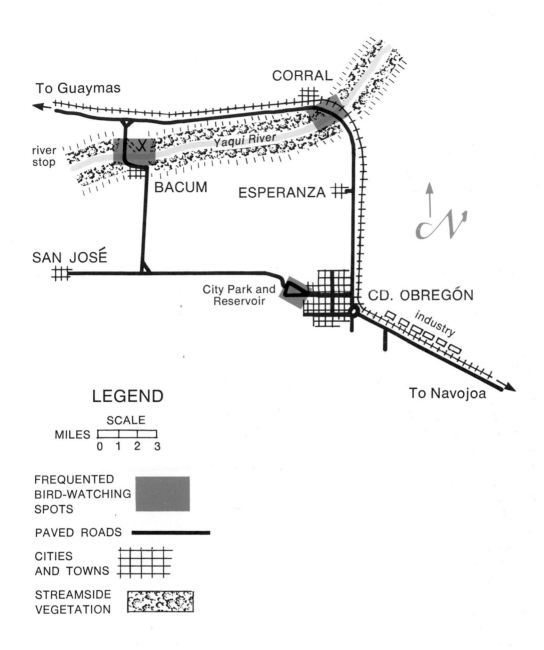

To Guaymas

CORRAL

river
stop

Yaqui River

BACUM

ESPERANZA

SAN JOSÉ

City Park and
Reservoir

CD. OBREGÓN

industry

To Navojoa

N

LEGEND

SCALE

MILES
0 1 2 3

FREQUENTED
BIRD-WATCHING
SPOTS

PAVED ROADS

CITIES
AND TOWNS

STREAMSIDE
VEGETATION

CIUDAD OBREGÓN, SONORA

Green-tailed Towhee   C*
Brown Towhee   R
Lark Sparrow   C
White-crowned Sparrow   A*
Lincoln's Sparrow   O*

You may go back to the main highway from here or continue on the shortcut through the little town of Bacum. Outside of town you will come to a fork. Turn left (east) towards the distant grain elevators of Obregón. This is lush cropland country, where you can safely stop along the road to watch for birds. Hordes of Bronzed Cowbirds can be seen in this area.

As you enter Obregón on the road from Bacum you will come upon a reservoir in the center of a green city park. Various waterbirds show up at this man-made lake, including Eared Grebes, Olivaceous Cormorants, Gadwalls, American Widgeons, Shovelers, Redheads, Ring-necked Ducks, Canvasbacks, Lesser Scaups, Buffleheads, Ring-billed Gulls, Bonaparte's Gulls, Gull-billed Terns, Forster's Terns, and Caspian Terns. The little stream beside the picnic area attracts Allen's and Violet-crowned Hummingbirds and Lesser Goldfinches in the autumn.

To pick up Highway 15 southeast out of town, stay on Calle Guerrero, the paved road which leaves the park, and drive due east through the city. Highway 15 intersects this road three blocks north of a rotary with a fountain. As you continue southward, cultivated fields line the road until they are suddenly replaced by thick desert growth dominated by saguaro, cardón, and organ pipe cactus interspersed with palo verde.

This is as far south as you will see wintering Sage Thrashers. The chief bird of interest on this stretch is the Mexican Crow, a few of which may be perched on telephone poles in the desert. As soon as you enter the green Mayo River Valley, Mexican Crows will become quite common.

Navojoa lies just beyond the bridge over the Mayo River. The river is backed up behind Mocúzari dam, about twenty-five miles upstream. Its waters are diverted into canals which support the vast irrigated tracts between Navajoa and the Gulf of California. The river bed is grassy, watered by a small stream and occasional ponds, and the banks are flanked by tall cottonwood trees. Bird watching is quite good along the river bed, and two Navojoa motels are located near the river. However, many species common to the Fuerte Valley do not live in this area, a fact which discourages most bird watchers from spending much time here.

Route 19: Alamos Sidetrip

Sonora Route 19 goes east to the quaint town of Alamos. You will see it branching off to your left (east) as you leave Navojoa. This paved road travels through desert vegetation into a sampling of tropical deciduous forest. This new vegetation is characterized by short, thin trees which form a "thorn jungle," and includes many flowering trees such as the pink Amapa. The huge pods of the kapok tree stand out on the hillsides as you pass below the Sierra de Alamos.

Although the trip involves only about forty minutes, you will most likely be detained by at least one group of large, very long-tailed blue birds sailing across the road. In addition to these Magpie-Jays, you will see many other interesting birds as you approach the thicker part of the forest. Hawks can become a nuisance, and you would do well to keep an eye out for the following species: Sharp-shinned, Cooper's, Red-tailed, Swainson's, Zone-tailed, White-tailed, Gray, Harris', Black, Marsh, Caracara, and Sparrow Hawks, in addition to both vultures. Many neotropical birds can be observed on the hillsides. Among the more conspicuous are Elegant Quail, Red-billed Pigeons, White-fronted Doves, and occa-

WADING AND GAME BIRDS

immature

adult

Boat-billed Heron
Cochlearius cochlearius

Bare-throated Tiger Heron
Tigrisoma mexicanum

Ruddy Ground Dove
Columbigallina talpa coti

Rufescent
Tinamou
*Crypturellus
cinnamomeus*

Elegant Quail
Lophortyx douglasii

Collared Plover
Charadrius collaris

Rufous-necked
Wood Rail
Aramides axillaris

Ruddy Quail Dove
Geotrygon montana

Rufous-bellied Chachalaca
Ortalis wagleri

sional morning and evening groups of noisy White-fronted Parrots.

Alamos, now a national monument, is an ancient, quiet town. Lately many American families have been converting its stately ruins into elegant homes. The interior court- yards of the homes and the two inns in town are full of flowers and trees which harbor a number of such wandering birds as Violet-crowned and Broad-billed Hummingbirds, Blue-rumped Parrotlets, Social Flycatchers, Scarlet-headed and Hooded Orioles, and House Finches.

Alamos is wedged between two normally-dry washes. Some trees grow on the wash banks, supported by ground water. Take early morning walks along these banks to see many of the area's common birds.

* * *

Several short trips near town provide good morning bird watching. Leave town west on Route 19. A dirt road branches to the right (north) just after the second bridge. Park here and stroll down the dirt road through riparian and hillside habitats and large weedy fields. Among the birds to look for along the wash are Elegant Quail, Red-billed Pigeons, Blue-rumped Parrotlets, White-fronted Parrots, Groove-billed Anis, Thick-billed Kingbirds, Social Flycatchers, Magpie-Jays, Happy Wrens, Scarlet-headed Orioles, Yellow Grosbeaks (summer), Varied Buntings, and Rufous-winged Sparrows.

Another good locality is a trailer park and ranch on the east side of town. Take the only dirt road east out of Alamos and follow the signs to the park. Your road will cross the Alamos Wash, some residential properties, and a cemetery. The grounds around the trailer park are perfect for an early morning stroll, and many White-fronted Parrots, numerous finches, and occasional distant Military Macaws can be seen during the autumn.

* * *

The best area for observing truly Mexican species in the state of Sonora is along the Rio Cuchujaqui. Unfortunately it can be reached only by several fairly rough dirt roads. It is not recommended that you take this trip on your own by automobile. Both inns at Alamos provide guides who will take you there in pickup trucks. If you do not hire a guide, try to get a local person to join you to point out the turns. Remember that there are no facilities of any sort once you leave Alamos.

The Rio Cuchujaqui and its small tributaries are lined with water cypress, thick shrubbery, and an occasional wild fig or palm tree. The hillsides support a heavy thorn forest, with many tall hairbrush cacti. During the greater part of the year the river consists of deep ponds and a bubbling stream which cuts its way through small gorges between rocks and flows over intervening sandy level stretches.

The shortest route to the river runs southward past a school for about seven miles, branching left at the major fork. This road will bring you to a section of the river that runs at a lower elevation and hosts more lowland species.

A longer route is a logging road from the pine country of Chihuahua which goes east out of town past the cemetery. A rough dirt road turns right (south) at the top of a hill and takes you to a narrow stream which abounds with birds.

If you stay on the logging road to Chihuahua, you will arrive at the river a little over an hour after leaving Alamos. There are many species in this area, and it is often surprisingly cool. If you have the time, ford the shallow stream and continue inland for about forty minutes until the road crosses the stream again. Here you may find more highland species, such as Hepatic Tanagers, and even chance upon a Solitary Eagle.

Alamos lies near the northern limit of the ranges of quite a few neo-tropical birds, and many species are quite local or erratic. These birds supplement the strange mixture of desert, tropical and highland species which co-exist in this area.

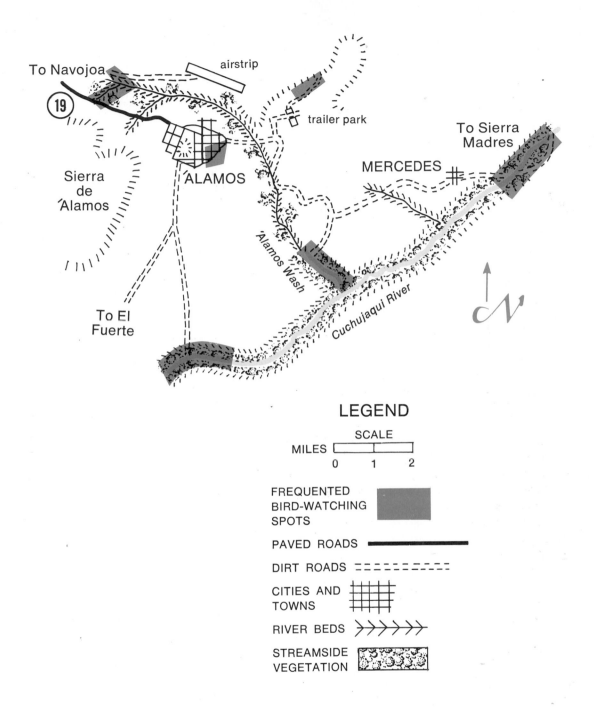

To Navojoa

⑲

airstrip

Sierra
de
Álamos

ALAMOS

trailer park

MERCEDES

To Sierra
Madres

Álamos Wash

To El
Fuerte

Cuchujaqui River

N

LEGEND

SCALE

MILES 0 1 2

FREQUENTED
BIRD-WATCHING
SPOTS

PAVED ROADS

DIRT ROADS

CITIES AND
TOWNS

RIVER BEDS

STREAMSIDE
VEGETATION

ALAMOS, SONORA

Birds of Alamos and the Rio Cuchujaqui

Note: When the symbol indicates abundance along the Rio Cuchujaqui only, it will be followed by the note "Rio." In most cases you can assume that a bird so marked has not been found around the town of Alamos.

Least Grebe   R   (*Rio*)
Olivaceous Cormorant   C   (*Rio*)
Great Blue Heron   O*   (*Rio*)
Green Heron   O   (*Rio*)
Common Egret   R   (*Rio*)
Snowy Egret   R   (*Rio*)
Bare-throated Tiger Heron   R   (*Rio, January record*)
Wood Ibis   X   (*Rio, October 1964*)
Gadwall   O*
Cinnamon Teal   O*   (*Rio*)
Green-winged Teal   O*   (*Rio*)
American Widgeon   O*   (*Rio*)
Lesser Scaup   C*   (*Rio*)
Turkey Vulture   A
Black Vulture   A
Sharp-shinned Hawk   C*
Cooper's Hawk   O*
Red-tailed Hawk   A
Swainson's Hawk   O   (*migration*)
Zone-tailed Hawk   O
White-tailed Hawk   O   (*spring best*)
Gray Hawk   O
Harris' Hawk   R
Black Hawk   R   (*nests along the Rio*)
Solitary Eagle   X   (*Rio, December 1964*)
Marsh Hawk   R*
Caracara   C
Pigeon Hawk   R   (*November record*)
Sparrow Hawk   A
Rufous-bellied Chachalaca   R
Elegant Quail   C
Common Snipe   R*   (*Rio*)
Spotted Sandpiper   A*   (*Rio*)
Greater Yellowlegs   R*
Red-billed Pigeon   C   (*R in winter*)
White-winged Dove   A
Mourning Dove   A
Ground Dove   A
Inca Dove   A
White-fronted Dove   C
Military Macaw   O

Blue-rumped Parrotlet   C   (*huge flocks in Alamos*)
White-fronted Parrot   A
Lilac-crowned Parrot   C   (*Rio chiefly*)
Mangrove Cuckoo   X   (*June 1965*)
Roadrunner   O
Lesser Roadrunner   R   (*rock bluffs*)
Groove-billed Ani   R
Elf Owl   R   (*April records*)
Ferruginous Owl   O
Great Horned Owl   R
Vaux's Swift   C   (*migration*)
White-throated Swift   R
Costa's Hummingbird   R   (*January records*)
Plain-capped Star-throat   O   (*spring best*)
Rivoli's Hummingbird   R   (*October records*)
Blue-throated Hummingbird   R   (*October records*)
Berylline Hummingbird   R   (*Rio, April records*)
Violet-crowned Hummingbird   C
Broad-billed Hummingbird   A
Coppery-tailed Trogon   O   (*spring best*)
Belted Kingfisher   C   (*Rio*)
Green Kingfisher   O   (*Rio*)
Russet-crowned Motmot   R   (*Rio*)
Red-shafted Flicker   C*
Gilded Flicker   A
Gila Woodpecker   A
Yellow-bellied Sapsucker   R*   (*Rio*)
Ladder-backed Woodpecker   A
Tropical Kingbird   O
Western Kingbird   O
Cassin's Kingbird   A
Thick-billed Kingbird   A
Social Flycatcher   C
Kiskadee Flycatcher   R
Sulphur-bellied Flycatcher   C   (*summer*)
Wied's Crested Flycatcher   R

Ash-throated Flycatcher   A*
Pale-throated Flycatcher   C
Olivaceous Flycatcher   C
Black Phoebe   A   (*Rio*)
Say's Phoebe   O*
Empidonax, species   A
Western Flycatcher   C*
Buff-breasted Flycatcher   R   (*November records*)
Tufted Flycatcher   C*   (*Rio*)
Coues' Flycatcher   C*
Western Wood Pewee   R   (*migration*)
Olive-sided Flycatcher   R   (*April migration*)
Vermilion Flycatcher   A
Beardless Flycatcher   O   (*Rio*)
Violet-Green Swallow   A   (*migration*)
Rough-winged Swallow   C
Purplish-backed Jay   O
Magpie-Jay   A
Mexican Crow   C   (*spring*)
Common Raven   A
Bridled Titmouse   R*   (*Rio*)
Verdin   A
House Wren   C*
Bar-vented Wren   R   (*Rio*) (*Sinaloa Wren*)
Happy Wren   O
Cactus Wren   C
Canyon Wren   O
Rock Wren   C
Mockingbird   A
Blue Mockingbird   O   (*Rio*)
Bendire's Thrasher   R
Curve-billed Thrasher   C
Robin   R   (*Rio, April records*)
Rufous-backed Robin   O
Hermit Thrush   O*
Orange-billed Nightingale-Thrush   X   (*Rio, January 1966*)
Brown-backed Solitaire   R*   (*Rio*)
Blue-Gray Gnatcatcher   A*
Black-capped Gnatcatcher   O
Ruby-crowned Kinglet   O*
Water Pipit   R*
Phainopepla   C
Loggerhead Shrike   A
Hutton's Vireo   R*   (*Rio*)
Bell's Vireo   C   (*spring best*)

Solitary Vireo   O*
Yellow-Green Vireo   O   (*summer*)
Warbling Vireo   O*
Orange-crowned Warbler   A*
Nashville Warbler   C   (*migration*)
Virginia's Warbler   O
Olive-backed Warbler   R   (*summer*)
Yellow Warbler   O*
Audubon's Warbler   O*
Black-throated Gray Warbler   R*
Louisiana Waterthrush   X   (*Rio, December 1965*)
MacGillivray's Warbler   R*
Yellowthroat   R   (*Rio, April records*)
Hooded Warbler   X   (*Rio, January 1966*)
Wilson's Warbler   A*
Painted Redstart   C*   (*Rio*)
Slate-throated Redstart   R*   (*Rio*)
Meadowlark, species   R
Yellow-headed Blackbird   R   (*October record*)
Hooded Oriole   A
Scarlet-headed Oriole   A
Black-vented Oriole   C
Bullock's Oriole   R   (*migration*)
Boat-tailed Grackle   R
Brown-headed Cowbird   C*
Western Tanager   R   (*migration*)
Hepatic Tanager   R*   (*Rio*)
Summer Tanager   O   (*except winter*)
Cardinal   A
Pyrrhuloxia   A
Yellow Grosbeak   O   (*summer*)
Black-headed Grosbeak   C*
Blue Grosbeak   C   (*autumn best*)
Lazuli Bunting   O*
Varied Bunting   C   (*spring best*)
Painted Bunting   R   (*autumn*)
Purple Finch   X   (*December 1965*)
House Finch   A
Lesser Goldfinch   C
Green-tailed Towhee   A*
Brown Towhee   A
Grasshopper Sparrow   R   (*autumn*)
Vesper Sparrow   A*
Lark Sparrow   A
Five-striped Sparrow   R

Rufous-winged Sparrow   C
Chipping Sparrow   A*
Clay-colored Sparrow   O*

Brewer's Sparrow   O*
White-crowned Sparrow   A*
Lincoln's Sparrow   R*   (*Rio*)

ROUTE 15: NAVOJOA TO SONORA-SINALOA STATELINE

AFTER LEAVING NAVOJOA on Route 15 South you will pass through several miles of irrigated wheatlands. In winter you may find large flocks of Lark Buntings beside the road.

When you re-enter the desert you will notice that it gradually thickens to thorn forest dominated by the giant cardón cactus. The birdlife does not change noticeably, although Black Hawks are more likely to be seen. This stretch seems to be the center of Caracara abundance. Up to fifty birds per hour of driving is not unusual. In the morning a few White-fronted Parrots may be seen winging their way from the coastal mangroves to the Alamos district. Seasonal roadside ponds on your right (west) may host Willets, Black-necked Stilts, American Avocets, Bonaparte's Gulls, and Black Phoebes.

CHAPTER III

SINALOA

Route 15: Sonora-Sinaloa Stateline to the Fuerte Valley

At the point where the Ferrocarril del Pacifico's tracks branch away from the road, you enter the long state of Sinaloa. Much of the rich desert vegetation in this area will be gone soon, for plans have been made to channel waters from the Rio Fuerte for irrigation of this vast plain. Already *ejidos* (communal ranches) have been set up, and the residents are busy clearing away the cardón cacti and dense shrubs.

Just beyond a new town set up by the government's ejido program, the road passes within several miles of the ocean, but the only evidence of its proximity is a little muddy creek bed which is sometimes filled with water. Look for Mangrove Swallows skimming over the water. In the creek bed and at several nearby seasonal roadside ponds you may find Eared Grebes, Least Grebes, Pied-billed Grebes, herons, Gadwalls, Shovelers, Cinnamon Teals, Lesser Scaups, Common Goldeneyes (rare), Ruddy Ducks, shorebirds, including dow-

itchers and Stilt Sandpipers, American Avocets, and Black-necked Stilts. Most of these birds can only be seen during the winter months.

A short distance beyond the creek, a tall hill rises on the east side of the highway. When irrigation brings prosperity, the village of Cerro Prieto at the base of the hill may become a booming city. Now, however, it is a quiet place with no tourist accommodations. There is a small pond just beyond the hill where you can usually see some birds.

After going through more thick thorn forest, you will approach a range of hills. Look for Harris' Hawks, Caracaras, Elegant Quail (during the wet season), Costa's Hummingbirds, Sulphur-bellied Flycatchers (summer), Verdins, Phainopeplas, and Gray Vireos (winter) around the bases of the hills. After winding through four more miles of hill country, you will suddenly see the vast green valley of the Fuerte River stretched out below you.

Route 15 to Sinaloa 23 Junction: the Fuerte Valley

This valley is the northern limit of many neotropical birds, for it is nearly perennially without frost. Many other species which do dwell in the Yaqui and Mayo valleys become much more prominent here. For the next

sixty miles, you will travel through a wide variety of agricultural landscapes, including fields of garden vegetables, cotton, and sugar cane.

As you approach the river on the northern edge of the valley, you may want to turn right (west) on a dirt road. This road follows a canal bordered by interesting streamside trees. In the weedy pond to your right (north) you may find Least Grebes.

The dirt road which branches south near the pond parallels the highway for a hundred yards, then ends beside a permanent pond under tall trees beside the river. Species you may find here include White-fronted Parrots, Violet-crowned Hummingbirds, Social Flycatchers, Kiskadee Flycatchers, Verdins, Happy Wrens, Bell's Vireos, Northern Waterthrushes (winter), Grayish Saltators, Summer Tanagers, Lesser Goldfinches, and wintering Clay-colored Sparrows. The Rio Fuerte, like other west coast rivers, has been reduced to a mere trickle, its waters rechanneled into irrigation ditches.

Return to Highway 15 and continue southeast until you come to the intersection of Sinaloa 23. During this seven-mile drive, check the roadside ponds on your right for Least Grebes, Olivaceous Cormorants, Black-necked Stilts, Groove-billed Anis, Kiskadees, Mangrove Swallows, and Scarlet-headed Orioles. This is as far north as Cattle Egrets have been seen at this writing.

When you reach the Route 23 intersection, you have several alternatives. Highway 15 continues southeast to Culiacán. The left branch of Route 23 leads northeast to Charay and San Blas, offering excellent riparian bird watching along the way. The right branch travels southwest to Los Mochis and on to the bay at Topolobampo. All three routes take you into good bird watching territory.

Los Mochis and Topolobampo

Los Mochis is a boom city, the focal point of the Fuerte Valley, destined to become one of the largest Mexican cities in the near future. It is located several miles southwest of Route 15, but large signs and a big rotary will not allow you to miss the turnoff. This is the major boulevard of Los Mochis. It will take you past the Santa Anita Hotel, which often has Barn Owls roosting on its roof at night. A major intersection marks the block on which the hotel is located. A left (southeast) turn will take you to Topolobampo, while a right (northwest) turn will take you past the ruins of the old Johnson estate, the former home of a prosperous American sugar king. The grounds have been preserved as botanical gardens, and many birds can be seen in the trees and flowers. Look for Gambel's Quail, Blue-rumped Parrotlets, Violet-crowned Hummingbirds, Social Flycatchers, Kiskadee Flycatchers, Wied's Crested Flycatchers, Coues' Flycatchers (winter), Western Wood Pewees (migration), Happy Wrens, Cedar Waxwings (winter), Black-throated Gray Warblers (winter), Lucy's Warblers (migra-

tion), American Redstarts (winter), Scarlet-headed Orioles, and Grayish Saltators.

The Topolobampo area is a half hour drive from Los Mochis. Route 23 is paved and passes through miles of sugar cane. Birds here include Wilson's Phalaropes (late summer), Black Terns (migration), and lines of Black-bellied and Fulvous Tree Ducks, geese, and flying ducks. In the winter you may find Grasshopper Sparrows and Clay-colored Sparrows feeding beside the road. Look for Burrowing Owls near pipes in the salty flats.

Before you cross the railroad tracks a few miles before the port, a dirt road heads off towards the ocean. It is quite rough, but it passes through some good mangroves. It ends at a dock where you can pay a peso and take a ten minute boat trip to a sandy beach. This beach has refreshment stands and is the home of many shorebirds, including both boobies, which rest on the beach itself.

Route 23 passes some mangrove trees just before reaching town. These host some waterbirds and the Mangrove Warbler.

Before you enter town you may wish to turn right (west) towards the Gulf on a road which winds around the outskirts of town. It will take you past a shrimp plant and provide a short scenic drive. The road deadends on the straits where you can get a fine view of the area and have a chance to scan for flying birds and leaping porpoises.

If you take Route 23 straight into town, you will quickly arrive at a main docking facility, a good place to study gulls, terns,

and Brown Boobies. A dirt road going left from the docks leads off to the left (northeast) around the bay to the Yacht Hotel. Here you can scan the mudflats for shorebirds and peruse vast Ohuira Bay for pelicans, Magnificent Frigatebirds, cormorants, boobies, ducks, Ospreys, gulls, terns, Black Skimmers, Green Kingfishers, and Mangrove Swallows. Black-bellied Tree Ducks fly by in long lines on some evenings.

Waterbirds of Ohuira and Topolobampo Bays

Common Loon   R*
Eared Grebe   C*
Red-billed Tropicbird   R   (*February record*)
White Pelican   C*   (*migration*)
Brown Pelican   A
Blue-footed Booby   C
Brown Booby   A
Double-crested Cormorant   A
Olivaceous Cormorant   C
Magnificent Frigatebird   A
Great Blue Heron   A
Green Heron   C
Little Blue Heron   A
Cattle Egret   X   (*October 1964*)
Reddish Egret   C
Common Egret   A
Snowy Egret   A
Louisiana Heron   A
Black-crowned Night Heron   O
Yellow-crowned Night Heron   C
Wood Ibis   O
White-faced Ibis   O
White Ibis   A
Roseate Spoonbill   O
White-fronted Goose   C*
Snow Goose   R*
Black-bellied Tree Duck   C
Fulvous Tree Duck   R
Gadwall   A*
Pintail   A*
Green-winged Teal   A*
Blue-winged Teal   A*
Cinnamon Teal   C*

American Widgeon   A*
Shoveler   A*
Redhead   R*
Canvasback   R*
Lesser Scaup   A*
Bufflehead   O*
Ruddy Duck   R*
Osprey   A
Common Gallinule   C
American Coot   A*
American Oystercatcher   R
Semipalmated Plover   A*
Wilson's Plover   C
Killdeer   C
Black-bellied Plover   C*
Ruddy Turnstone   C*
Long-billed Curlew   A*
Whimbrel   A*
Spotted Sandpiper   A*
Willet   A
Greater Yellowlegs   A*
Lesser Yellowlegs   A*
Least Sandpiper   A*
Dunlin   R*
Dowitcher, species   A*
Western Sandpiper   C*
Marbled Godwit   A*
Sanderling   C*
American Avocet   A*
Black-necked Stilt   A
Wilson's Phalarope   C   (*migration*)
Glaucous-winged Gull   R*
Western Gull   A
Herring Gull   C*

California Gull   C*
Ring-billed Gull   A*
Laughing Gull   A   (*best in summer*)
Bonaparte's Gull   C*
Heermann's Gull   A
Gull-billed Tern   C
Forster's Tern   A*
Common Tern   C*

Least Tern   A   (*summer*)
Royal Tern   O
Elegant Tern   C
Caspian Tern   A
Black Tern   C   (*migration*)
Black Skimmer   C
Green Kingfisher   O
Mangrove Swallow   C

ISLA FARALLON

A TRIP to Isla Farallon will be of interest if you have time, money, and good weather. This island lies about twenty-five miles southwest of Topolobampo, rising from the ocean floor like the peak of a gigantic mountain. Reserve a boat at one of the larger hotels and allow at least six hours for the trip. Leave early, for the waters become quite choppy in the afternoon. Do not drink any liquids before leaving.

For the first hour of your trip, your boat will pass through Topolobampo Bay. Look for porpoises, long lines of wintering White-fronted Geese, and flocks of White Pelicans, Brown Boobies, Blue-footed Boobies, and Elegant Terns.

Isla Farallon lies about two hours beyond the Bay. The sea teems with birdlife, and long lines of boobies, cormorants, pelicans, gulls, and terns fly overhead. About halfway out you should begin to see massive flocks of Northern Phalaropes interspersed with Red Phalaropes. Black Petrels and Least Petrels will wing above the water in their peculiar, bat-like manner. Occasionally you will see a jaeger harassing gulls and terns. In the winter thousands of Bonaparte's Gulls feed on tiny marine organisms. Ask your captain to pass close by any shrimp or fishing boats you may see. Many pelagic birds, including Sooty Shearwaters, may be attracted by their refuse.

As you approach Isla Farallon, you can look forward to your first glimpse of the Red-billed Tropicbird. About fifty pairs of these long-tailed, graceful birds nest here. They may fly close to your boat—certainly you will see them sailing about in the updrafts over the island. Many thousands of Brown Boobies and Blue-footed Boobies also make their homes on Isla Farallon. Sea lions add their harsh barking to the screams of the seabirds.

Birds at and about Isla Farallon

Common Loon   O*
Eared Grebe   A*
Pink-footed Shearwater   R   (*summer*)
Sooty Shearwater   O   (*summer*)
Black Petrel   A
Least Petrel   C   (*spring*)
Red-billed Tropic-bird   A   (*around Isla Farallon only*)
Brown Pelican   A
Blue-footed Booby   A
Brown Booby   A

Double-crested Cormorant   A
Magnificent Frigate-bird   A
Spotted Sandpiper   C*   (*on Isla Farallon only*)
Wandering Tattler   R   (*May record*)
Red Phalarope   C*
Northern Phalarope   A*
Pomarine Jaeger   R   (*April, 1967*)
Parasitic Jaeger   R   (*December, 1967*)
Western Gull   A
Herring Gull   C*

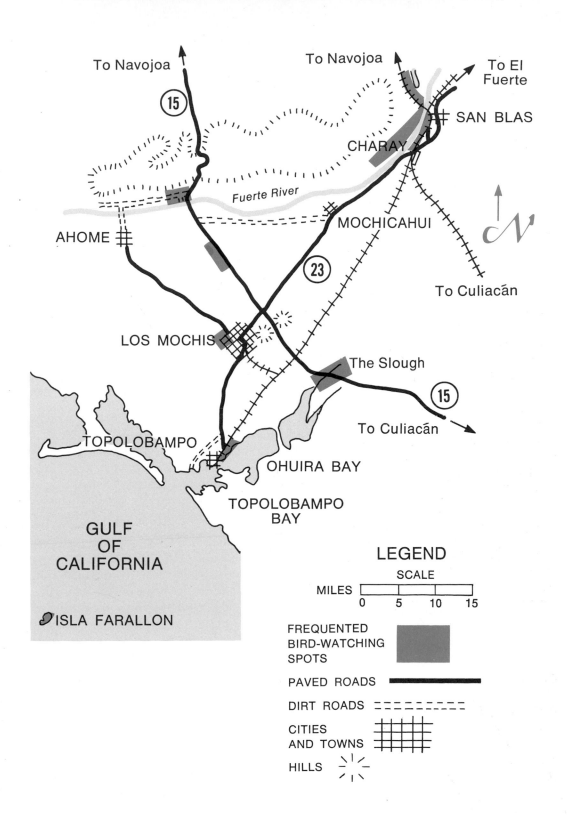

To Navojoa

To Navojoa

To El Fuerte

(15)

SAN BLAS

CHARAY

Fuerte River

AHOME

MOCHICAHUI

(23)

To Culiacán

LOS MOCHIS

The Slough

(15)

To Culiacán

TOPOLOBAMPO

OHUIRA BAY

TOPOLOBAMPO BAY

GULF OF CALIFORNIA

ISLA FARALLON

N

LEGEND

SCALE

MILES

0   5   10   15

FREQUENTED BIRD-WATCHING SPOTS

PAVED ROADS

DIRT ROADS

CITIES AND TOWNS

HILLS

FUERTE VALLEY, SINALOA

California Gull   O*
Ring-billed Gull   C*
Laughing Gull   C
Franklin's Gull   R   (*April, 1967*)
Bonaparte's Gull   A*
Heermann's Gull   A

Sabine's Gull   X   (*May, 1968*)
Forster's Tern   C*
Common Tern   O*
Elegant Tern   A
Caspian Tern   O

ROUTE 23: LOS MOCHIS TOWARD SAN BLAS

A REALLY FINE BIRD WATCHING AREA can be reached from Los Mochis by taking Route 23 northeast towards San Blas and El Fuerte. After crossing the Route 15 intersection you will pass through vast sugar cane fields. In the spring and summer, conditions are right for many Fulvous Tree Ducks and a few Black-bellied Tree Ducks to feed. During these seasons they often can be seen flying across the road. Ground Chats and White-collared Seedeaters can be found in the tall grass and weeds beside the irrigated sugar cane fields during the summer months. Groove-billed Anis may be seen in the bushes and Elegant Quail can be sighted crossing the road.

At kilometer post 25 where Route 23 curves to the right, take the left (west) branch into the little canal-threaded village of Charay. Dirt roads follow both sides of most of the canals. Turn left (northwest) off the main street when you reach the plaza, crossing the main canal. This will become a dirt road which takes you straight to the Fuerte River in about a mile. Birds are quite abundant along the road. A banana plantation lies behind a barb-wire fence on the left (south) side. Look for Gray Hawks, Blue-rumped Parrotlets (feeding in the weeds in the winter), White-fronted Parrots (during early morning hours), Plain-capped Star-throats, Violet-crowned Hummingbirds, Broad-billed Hummingbirds, Happy Wrens, Blue Mockingbirds (in thick shrubbery under tall trees), Yellow-Green Vireos (in summer in the forest on the left), Scarlet-headed Orioles, Grayish Saltators, and many flycatchers.

The road passes a small pond on the left, then goes through a grove of tall trees which host nesting Rose-throated Becards and hordes of Social Flycatchers. Drier areas dotted with Guaymuchil trees and mesquite bushes lie beyond the grove. Look for Rufous-winged Sparrows, Varied Buntings, and other desert birds.

The road forks to the right in two places. Either of these righthand forks will take you to the low diversion dam on the river. Tall cottonwoods line the banks, backed by mixtures of shrubbery, scattered cornfields, and occasional ponds. By walking northeast along the river past this dam and the next one to the railroad bridge at San Blas, you can easily see between one and two hundred species a day, including many waterbirds.

* * *

Another good riparian birdwatching spot can be reached by taking Route 23 from Charay towards the town of San Blas. After crossing the railroad tracks near the new station (which has a restaurant), continue around the high hill and take the old road that branches left (northwest). Take another left on the first dirt road. This road crosses the railroad tracks on a dangerous curve just before reaching the second reservoir. This is an elevated area, a good spot for scanning for waterbirds.

When high water is not crossing over the dam, you can drive or walk to the opposite shore and walk up stream. Bare-throated Tiger Herons and a Black-collared Hawk have been seen beside the river.

* * *

Back on Route 23, the town of San Blas lies a mile to the northeast. The twenty-eight mile stretch of road from San Blas to El Fuerte has not proved good for bird watching.

Birds of the El Fuerte River, Charay

Eared Grebe   A*
Least Grebe   C
Pied-billed Grebe   C*
Olivaceous Cormorant   A
Anhinga   R
Great Blue Heron   A
Green Heron   C
Little Blue Heron   O
Common Egret   C
Snowy Egret   C
Louisiana Heron   R
Bare-throated Tiger Heron   O
White Ibis   C
Roseate Spoonbill   R
Black-bellied Tree Duck   C
Fulvous Tree Duck   O
Mallard   O*
Gadwall   A*
Pintail   A*
Green-winged Teal   A*
Blue-winged Teal   A*
Cinnamon Teal   A*
American Widgeon   A*
Shoveler   A*
Ring-necked Duck   C*
Lesser Scaup   C*
Common Goldeneye   R*   (*February records*)
Bufflehead   O*
Ruddy Duck   A*
Turkey Vulture   A
Black Vulture   A
Sharp-shinned Hawk   C*
Cooper's Hawk   C*
Red-tailed Hawk   C
Red-shouldered Hawk   X   (*April 1967*)
Gray Hawk   C
Black-collared Hawk   X   (*February 1963*)
Black Hawk   O
Great Black Hawk   R
Blackish Crane Hawk   X   (*April 1967*)

Laughing Falcon   X   (*February 1963*)
Caracara   A
Peregrine Falcon   R*
Sparrow Hawk   C
Rufous-bellied Chachalaca   R
Gambel's Quail   O
Elegant Quail   C
Common Gallinule   O
American Coot   A*
Killdeer   A
Common Snipe   O*
Spotted Sandpiper   A*
Solitary Sandpiper   O*
Greater Yellowlegs   A*
Lesser Yellowlegs   A*
Least Sandpiper   A*
Dowitcher, species   A*
American Avocet   C*
Black-necked Stilt   A
Ring-billed Gull   C*
Bonaparte's Gull   R*
Forster's Tern   O*
Red-billed Pigeon   C
White-winged Dove   A
Mourning Dove   A
Ground Dove   A
Inca Dove   A
White-fronted Dove   O
Military Macaw   R   (*March records*)
Blue-rumped Parrotlet   A
White-fronted Parrot   A
Yellow-billed Cuckoo   O
Roadrunner   R
Groove-billed Ani   O
Great Horned Owl   O
Plain-capped Star-throat   C
Violet-crowned Hummingbird   A
Broad-billed Hummingbird   A
Belted Kingfisher   A*
Green Kingfisher   A   (*on low branches over the river and canals*)
Red-shafted Flicker   C*

Gilded Flicker   C
Gila Woodpecker   A
Yellow-bellied Sapsucker   R*
Ladder-backed Woodpecker   A
Rose-throated   Becard   C   (*in   cotton-
  woods*)
Tropical Kingbird   A
Western Kingbird   C*
Cassin's Kingbird   A
Thick-billed Kingbird   A
Social Flycatcher   A
Kiskadee Flycatcher   A
Wied's Crested Flycatcher   C
Ash-throated/Nutting's   Flycatcher   O
Olivaceous Flycatcher   C
Black Phoebe   A
Say's Phoebe   R*
Empidonax, species   A*
Gray Flycatcher   R*
Western Flycatcher   A*
White-throated Flycatcher   O
Coues' Flycatcher   O*
Western Wood Pewee   R   (*migration*)
Vermilion Flycatcher   A
Beardless Flycatcher   O
Violet-Green   Swallow   C   (*spring migra-
  tion*)
Tree Swallow   O*
Mangrove Swallow   A   (*over river*)
Rough-winged Swallow   A
Barn Swallow   C   (*migration*)
Cliff Swallow   O   (*migration*)
Purple Martin   R   (*migration*)
Magpie-Jay   O
Mexican Crow   A
Raven, species   A
Verdin   A
House Wren   A*
Bar-vented Wren   O
Happy Wren   A   (*elusive*)
Cactus Wren   A
Long-billed Marsh Wren   R*
Canyon Wren   O*
Rock Wren   O*
Mockingbird   A
Blue Mockingbird   O
Bendire's Thrasher   R
Curve-billed Thrasher   A

Rufous-backed Robin   C
Blue-Gray Gnatcatcher   A*
Ruby-crowned Kinglet   R*
Water Pipit   C*
Phainopepla   C
Loggerhead Shrike   A
Bell's Vireo   C   (*spring best*)
Gray Vireo   R*
Solitary Vireo   C*
Yellow-Green Vireo   C   (*summer*)
Warbling Vireo   C*
Black-and-White   Warbler   R
  (*migration*)
Worm-eating   Warbler   X   (*October,
  1965*)
Orange-crowned Warbler   A*
Nashville Warbler   C*
Olive-backed   Warbler   R   (*April records
  in cottonwoods*)
Yellow Warbler   O
Audubon's Warbler   A*
Black-throated Gray Warbler   A*
Yellow-throated   Warbler   X   (*May,
  1968*)
MacGillivray's Warbler   A*
Yellowthroat   O*
Ground Chat   O   (*summer*)
Yellow-breasted Chat   C
Wilson's Warbler   A*
American Redstart   R*
House Sparrow   A
Yellow-winged   Cacique   R   (*March
  record*)
Red-winged Blackbird   O
Orchard Oriole   C   (*summer*)
Hooded Oriole   O
Scarlet-headed Oriole   A
Bullock's Oriole   C   (*migration*)
Boat-tailed Grackle   A
Brown-headed Cowbird   A*
Bronzed Cowbird   A
Western Tanager   O   (*migration*)
Summer Tanager   O
Grayish Saltator   A
Cardinal   A
Pyrrhuloxia   A
Black-headed Grosbeak   C   (*migration*)
Indigo Bunting   R   (*migration*)

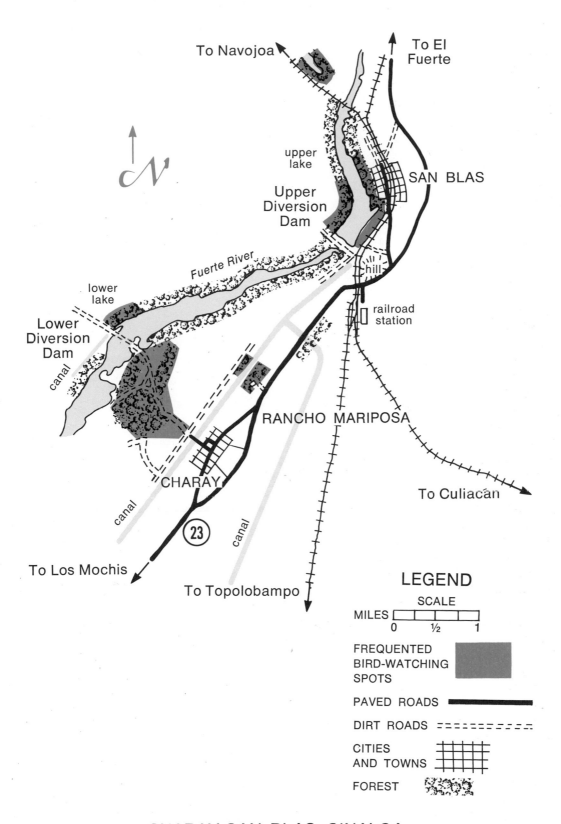

To Navojoa

To El Fuerte

upper lake

Upper Diversion Dam

SAN BLAS

Fuerte River

lower lake

Lower Diversion Dam

canal

hill

railroad station

RANCHO MARIPOSA

To Culiacan

CHARAY

canal

23

canal

To Los Mochis

To Topolobampo

LEGEND

SCALE

MILES

0   ½   1

FREQUENTED BIRD-WATCHING SPOTS

PAVED ROADS

DIRT ROADS

CITIES AND TOWNS

FOREST

CHARAY-SAN BLAS, SINALOA

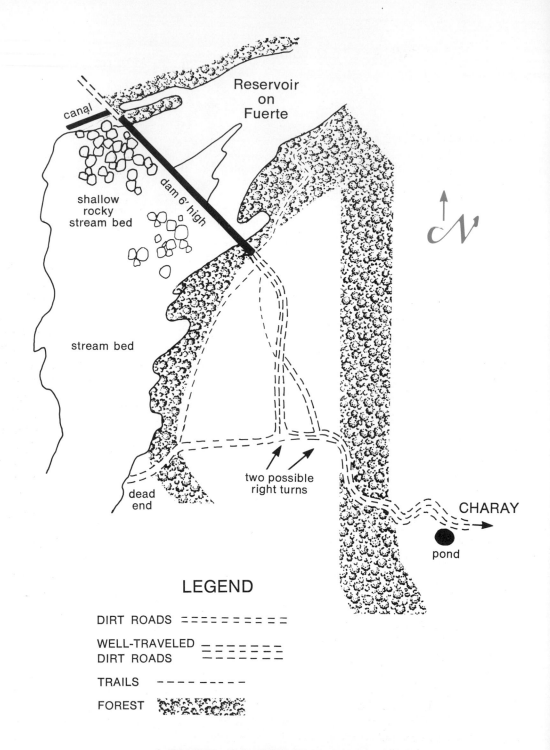

Reservoir on Fuerte

canal

dam 6' high

shallow rocky stream bed

stream bed

two possible right turns

dead end

CHARAY

pond

N

LEGEND

DIRT ROADS ========= == =

WELL-TRAVELED ======== =
DIRT ROADS ======== =

TRAILS - - - - - - - -

FOREST

LOWER DIVERSION DAM AREA
Charay, Sinaloa

Lazuli Bunting   A*
Varied Bunting   A
Painted Bunting   C   (*migration*)
House Finch   A
Lesser Goldfinch   A
Green-tailed Towhee   A*
Brown Towhee   C
Lark Bunting   R*
Grasshopper Sparrow   R*
Vesper Sparrow   R*

Lark Sparrow   A*
Rufous-winged Sparrow   A
Black-throated Sparrow   C*
Chipping Sparrow   A*
Clay-colored Sparrow   C*
Brewer's Sparrow   O*
White-crowned Sparrow   A*
Golden-crowned   Sparrow   X   (*October 1965*)
Lincoln's Sparrow   C*

ROUTE 15: SINALOA 23 JUNCTION TO CULIACÁN

RETURN ON ROUTE 23 southwest to the junction of Mexico 15. Turn left (southeast) towards Culiacán. The road will take you through mile after mile of irrigated farmlands planted in sugar cane, cotton, and vegetables and some banana, citrus, papaya, and mango orchards. Many industries related to agricultural processing attract immense numbers of doves, blackbirds (wintering Yellow-headed, Red-winged and Brewer's), Boat-tailed Grackles, cowbirds (Brown-headed and Bronzed), wintering Lark Buntings and sparrows. Take note of any fields which are being flooded, for they attract numerous waterbirds.

Among the birds you may find along this stretch of highway are flocks of Cattle Egrets (up to 500), Common and Snowy Egrets, White Ibis, and Black-bellied and Fulvous Tree Ducks. During migration periods you may also see White-faced Ibis (up to 300), shorebirds (including large groups of Whimbrels), Ring-billed Gulls, and massive flocks of swallows (Tree, Barn, and Bank). To find where White-fronted and Snow Geese are feeding, consult with hunters or guides at one of the hotels in Los Mochis. Check for White-tailed Hawks and other species near fires in the sugar cane. (Firing is done both to remove excess leaves from the cane stalks before they go to the mill and to drive out rodents.)

Less than ten miles from the Route 23 junction you will cross a bridge over a tidal estuary. You can park easily on both sides of the southern approach. Among the birds you may find here at proper seasons are Double-crested Cormorants, Olivaceous Cormorants, most herons, White-faced Ibis, Roseate Spoonbills, Black-bellied and Fulvous Tree-Ducks, Gadwalls, Pintails, all three teals, American Widgeons, Shovelers, Redheads, Lesser Scaups, Ruddy Ducks, Redbreasted Mergansers (rare), Ospreys, American Coots, many shorebirds (including Stilt Sandpiper), American Avocets, Black-necked Stilts, Wilson's Phalaropes (late April and late August), gulls, terns (including Gull-billed, Forster's, Common, Least, Royal, Caspian, and Black) and swallows (including Tree, Mangrove, Roughwinged, Barn, Bank, and Cliff).

Just before you reach the toll bridge over the Rio Sinaloa near Guasave, check the ponds on your right. These ponds have resident Least Grebe and during migration periods may host Solitary Sandpiper and Least Tern as well as the usual puddle birds. Cross the toll bridge and scan the river for Mangrove Swallows. Groove-billed Anis can be seen beside the road for the next few miles in the bushes or near cattle. Cassin's Kingbirds are commonly seen on the telephone wires here in the winter. You will re-enter the thorn forest before reaching Guaymuchil, the next major town. (Guaymuchil is named after a local pod tree, *Pithecellobium dulce,* the fruit of which is savored by parrots.)

Most of the route from Guaymuchil to

Culiacán passes through hilly country covered with dry-land farms and a combination of thorn forest and tropical deciduous forest. You will not find many birds along this stretch, although you should keep an eye out for Zone-tailed Hawks, Gray Hawks, Military Macaws (rare), Orange-fronted Parakeets, White-fronted Parrots, Thick-billed Kingbirds, Purplish-backed Jays, Magpie-Jays, hordes of Mexican Crows, and wintering Cassin's Sparrows. New canals are pushing through much of this area, although their waters are ultimately destined to flow onto the flat coastal plain to the west.

CULIACÁN

THE VAST, lush farmlands of the Culiacán Valley, the southernmost of the major irrigated valleys, are by-passed by Route 15. Culiacán is situated at the inland edge of the valley beside a large diversion dam. This dam backs up water for several miles near the city. The two tributaries of the Rio Culiacán are dammed upstream. Aquatic vegetation lines the banks of the rivers and provides good bird watching.

When you reach the outskirts of Culiacán, you will have to pay a toll to cross the elevated causeway and bridge. One of Culiacán's many overnight facilities is located on your left (east) immediately after you pass the toll booth. Its grounds provide good bird watching, as does the swamp on the west side of the road halfway down the causeway between the toll booth and the bridge. The early morning hours are especially good for finding birds in and near the swamp. The tall trees and shrubs are full of landbirds, and the surrounding marshes give refuge to many waterbirds. You may even see your first Jacana.

If you feel hardy and the insects are not too troublesome, hike along the cropland that flanks the swamp. A little thatched house to the left (south) of the swamp can be reached by taking a dirt road about thirty yards long. Noisy groups of tiny Blue-rumped Parrotlets and trees full of Rufous-backed Robins are often found around this dwelling. Weedy fields in the area often host Painted Buntings and White-collared Seedeaters. You may wish to continue walking to the Rio Culiacán, which is a haven for many ducks, American Coots, and swallows.

Birds of the Culiacán River Crossing

Least Grebe   C
Olivaceous Cormorant   O
Green Heron   O
Little Blue Heron   O
Cattle Egret   O
Common Egret   R
White-faced Ibis   O
Black-bellied Tree Duck   C
Pintail   O*
Shoveler   O*
Ruddy Duck   R*
Turkey Vulture   C
Black Vulture   A
Cooper's Hawk   R*
Caracara   R
Pigeon Hawk   R*

Common Gallinule   C
American Coot   A*
Jacana   C
Killdeer   A
Spotted Sandpiper   A*
Solitary Sandpiper   C*
Greater Yellowlegs   R*
Baird's Sandpiper   R   (*November record*)
Dowitcher, species   O*
Black-necked Stilt   O
Forster's Tern   R*
White-winged Dove   C
Mourning Dove   C
Ground Dove   A
Inca Dove   A
Blue-rumped Parrotlet   A

CUCKOOS, WOODPECKERS, WOODCREEPER

male

Pale-billed Woodpecker
Phloeoceastes guatemalensis

female

Rufous-rumped Ground Cuckoo
Morococcyx erythropygus

Ivory-billed
Woodcreeper
Xiphorhynchus flavigaster

male

Gray-crowned Woodpecker
Piculus auricularis

Squirrel Cuckoo
Piaya cayana

male

female

female

male

**Golden-cheeked
Woodpecker**
Centurus chrysogenys

Lineated Woodpecker
Dryocopus lineatus

Gray-crowned
Woodpecker
Piculus auricularis

Groove-billed Ani   C
Plain-capped Star-throat   C
Violet-crowned Hummingbird   C
Broad-billed Hummingbird   A
Belted Kingfisher   O*
Green Kingfisher   O
Gila Woodpecker   A
Rose-throated Becard   O   (*in cottonwood swamp*)
Tropical Kingbird   A
Cassin's Kingbird   C*
Thick-billed Kingbird   O
Social Flycatcher   A
Kiskadee Flycatcher   A
Black Phoebe   C
Say's Phoebe   O*
Coues' Flycatcher   C*
Vermilion Flycatcher   A
Tree Swallow   O*
Mangrove Swallow   C   (*over the river*)
Rough-winged Swallow   A
Barn Swallow   O   (*migration*)
Cliff Swallow   O   (*summer*)
Purple Martin   R   (*April record*)
Mexican Crow   A
House Wren   C*
Happy Wren   C   (*in cottonwood swamp*)
Mockingbird   A
Curve-billed Thrasher   R
Rufous-backed Robin   A
Blue-Gray Gnatcatcher   C*
Cedar Waxwing   O*
Loggerhead Shrike   C*
Solitary Vireo   C*
Warbling Vireo   O*
Black-and-White Warbler   R*
Orange-crowned Warbler   A*
Nashville Warbler   C*
Virginia's Warbler   O   (*migration*)
Lucy's Warbler   O*
Yellow Warbler   O
Audubon's Warbler   A*
Black-throated Gray Warbler   A*
Northern Waterthrush   R   (*migration*)
MacGillivray's Warbler   C*
Yellowthroat   R*
Yellow-breasted Chat   O
Wilson's Warbler   A*

American Redstart   R*
House Sparrow   A
Red-winged Blackbird   C
Orchard Oriole   C
Hooded Oriole   A
Scarlet-headed Oriole   A   (Streak-backed)
Bullock's Oriole   O*
Boat-tailed Grackle   A
Brewer's Blackbird   O*
Bronzed Cowbird   A
Pale-vented Euphonia   O   (*in cottonwood swamp*) (Scrub)
Western Tanager   O   (*April*)
Grayish Saltator   O   (*in cottonwood swamp*)
Cardinal   A
Pyrrhuloxia   C
Black-headed Grosbeak   O*
Blue Grosbeak   C
Varied Bunting   O
Painted Bunting   C
House Finch   A
White-collared Seedeater   A
Blue-Black Grassquit   A   (*best in summer*)
Lesser Goldfinch   C
Lark Sparrow   C*
Clay-colored Sparrow   C*
White-crowned Sparrow   A*
Lincoln's Sparrow   C*

Beyond the motel is a rotary intersection with a fountain. If you wish to pass through town, go three-quarters of the way around the rotary and follow the Route 15 signs through the city. Focal points for bird watchers are the trees and gardens which surround the elegant homes that line the river on the northwest side of town.

Another good spot is an area of grassy fields near the municipal airport. Reach it by turning onto Sinaloa Route 30 at the rotary. The airport is located about three miles down the road. Birds can be quite abundant in the fields when the weeds are in seed in the autumn. Look for Black Swifts, Ground Chats, Blue Grosbeaks, buntings (Indigo, Lazuli, Varied, and Painted), White-collared Seedeaters, Clay-colored Sparrows, and Grasshopper Sparrows. In the summer you may also find Yellow Grosbeaks in the valley. Elegant Quail are common in this area, although they are difficult to spot.

ROUTE 15: CULIACÁN TO MAZATLÁN

HIGHWAY 15 TRAVERSES the 144 miles to Mazatlán through somewhat tropical country. This stretch covers many low hills and is dry much of the year. Fairly heavy tropical deciduous forest blankets the hillsides, while unirrigated farms occupy the level land. Five small rivers thread the area, providing diversified habitats for various species.

Neither the giant cardón cactus nor the saguaro can be found in this area, although hairbrush cacti are interspersed among the hillside vegetation. This contrasts with the lowlands of Sonora where the various "tree" cacti tower above the shrubs. Notice that when the farmers here clear their fields they often leave hairbrush cacti standing along with occasional shade and flowering trees. Hawks, vultures, jays, flycatchers, and shrikes use these trees and cacti for perches.

Around kilometer post 1410, about six miles south of Culiacán, you may find flocks of huge White-naped Swifts flying overhead in late winter. Other birds to look for in this spot are Gray Hawks, Orange-fronted Parakeets, White-fronted Parrots, Black Swifts, Purplish-backed Jays, Magpie-Jays, and Rusty-crowned Ground Sparrows. You may also find flocks of Cattle Egrets in the fields. It is interesting to note that the first Cattle Egret found in western Mexico was sighted in some fields near here on March 22, 1964.

The Quelite River Valley, half hour north of Mazatlán is a fair place to study local birds. A dirt road turns right (west) just before a bridge a short distance beyond the turnoff west to Mármol. This road travels through diversified habitats and is ideal for bird watchers who like to hike through rough country. The stream in the area runs all year round, supporting rich vegetation along its banks and flowing into pools frequented by waterbirds.

A monument beside Highway 15 marks the Tropic of Cancer. The dense dry vegetation on the hillsides around it hosts several species. From December through April you should see White-naped Swifts on the wing. As you approach Mazatlán you will pass through orchards of mangos and some papayas. Within a wide radius of the city most trees have been cut for firewood, and only planted palm trees lend a tropical atmosphere.

Birds Between Culiacán and Mazatlán, Including the Quelite Valley

Least Grebe   O
Pied-billed Grebe   O*
White Pelican   R   (*in migrating flocks overhead*)
Olivaceous Cormorant   A
Anhinga   O
Great Blue Heron   C
Green Heron   A
Little Blue Heron   O
Cattle Egret   O
Common Egret   C

Snowy Egret   A
Louisiana Heron   O
White-faced Ibis   O
White Ibis   O
Gadwall   C*
Green-winged Teal   C*
Blue-winged Teal   C*
Cinnamon Teal   C*
American Widgeon   C*
Shoveler   C*
Turkey Vulture   A

Black Vulture   A

Sharp-shinned Hawk   C*

Cooper's Hawk   C*

Red-tailed Hawk   A

Swainson's Hawk   A   (*migration*)

Zone-tailed Hawk   O

Short-tailed Hawk   O

Gray Hawk   A

Harris' Hawk   C

Black Hawk   C

Marsh Hawk   O*

Caracara   A

Sparrow Hawk   A*

Rufous-bellied Chachalaca   R

Elegant Quail   C

Common Gallinule   O

American Coot   A*

Jacana   C

Killdeer   A

Common Snipe   R*

Spotted Sandpiper   O*

Greater Yellowlegs   C*

Least Sandpiper   C*

Dowitcher, species   O*

American Avocet   C*

Black-necked Stilt   C

Red-billed Pigeon   C

White-winged Dove   A

Mourning Dove   A*

Ground Dove   A

Inca Dove   A

White-fronted Dove   C

Orange-fronted Parakeet   C

Blue-rumped Parrotlet   O

White-fronted Parrot   A

Lilac-crowned Parrot   C

Yellow-billed Cuckoo   R   (*August rec-ords*)

Squirrel Cuckoo   R

Roadrunner   R

Groove-billed Ani   C

White-naped Swift   C   (*December–April*)

Black Swift   O   (*late winter*)

Plain-capped Star-throat   O

Cinnamon Hummingbird   C

Violet-crowned Hummingbird   R

Broad-billed Hummingbird   A

Citreoline Trogon   R   (*October record*)

Belted Kingfisher   O*

Green Kingfisher   O

Gila Woodpecker   A

Golden-cheeked Woodpecker   C

Ladder-backed Woodpecker   C

Tropical Kingbird   A

Western Kingbird   O*

Cassin's Kingbird   C*

Thick-billed Kingbird   A

Social Flycatcher   A

Kiskadee Flycatcher   C

Wied's Crested Flycatcher   C

Ash-throated/Nutting's Flycatcher   A

Olivaceous Flycatcher   C

Black Phoebe   C

Empidonax, species   A

Beardless Flycatcher   R

Vermilion Flycatcher   A*

Tree Swallow   C*

Mangrove Swallow   C   (*over rivers*)

Rough-winged Swallow   A

Barn Swallow   O   (*migration*)

Purplish-backed Jay   C   (*best in spring*)

Magpie-Jay   A

Common Raven   A

Mexican Crow   A

House Wren   C*

Happy Wren   C

Mockingbird   A

Blue Mockingbird   R

Curve-billed Thrasher   C

Rufous-backed Robin   C

Wood Thrush   X   (*January 1964 in Quel-ite Valley*)

Hermit Thrush   R*

Blue-Gray Gnatcatcher   A*

Water Pipit   R*

Cedar Waxwing   R*

Loggerhead Shrike   A*

Bell's Vireo   O

Solitary Vireo   C*

Yellow-Green Vireo   O   (*summer*)

Warbling Vireo   C*

Orange-crowned Warbler   A*

Nashville Warbler   C*

Olive-backed Warbler   O   (Trop. Parula)

Yellow Warbler   C*

Audubon's Warbler   A*

Black-throated Gray Warbler　A*
MacGillivray's Warbler　C*
Yellow-breasted Chat　C
Wilson's Warbler　A*
House Sparrow　A
Yellow-winged Cacique　O
Meadowlark, species　C*
Red-winged Blackbird　O
Orchard Oriole　O
Hooded Oriole　C
Scarlet-headed Oriole　A
Black-vented Oriole　O
Bullock's Oriole　C　(*migration*)
Boat-tailed Grackle　A
Brown-headed Cowbird　C*
Bronzed Cowbird　C
Summer Tanager　C
Grayish Saltator　O

Cardinal　A
Pyrrhuloxia　A
Yellow Grosbeak　R
Black-headed Grosbeak　C　(*migration*)
Blue Grosbeak　A
Indigo Bunting　C*
Lazuli Bunting　O*
Varied Bunting　A
Painted Bunting　C
House Finch　A
White-collared Seedeater　C*
Lesser Goldfinch　C
Green-tailed Towhee　C*
Rusty-crowned Ground Sparrow　R
Lark Sparrow　A*
Clay-colored Sparrow　C*
White-crowned Sparrow　A*
Lincoln's Sparrow　C*

Mazatlán

Mazatlán now rivals Acapulco as a luxury resort center. It is fast becoming a modern city with widespread suburban areas. Hotels and motels are plentiful, lining the beaches, dominating the main road into town, and even encroaching on the downtown residential areas.

The city is located on a hilly peninsula, and attractive rainbow colors adorn the hillside buildings. The ocean is the center of all activity. Huge freight and passenger liners, as well as the larger fishing boats occupy the south side of the harbor. Sport fishing facilities (including "booby boats"), and the homes of the wealthy can be found along the seaward peninsula to the west.

The scenic entry into town is via the paved road which branches right (west) off Highway 15 beyond the railroad tracks. This road is marked by the sign "Playas" and many beach hotel signs. It leads directly to the ocean, and Cattle Egrets are often seen along it. Later this road joins Olas Altas, the main coastal boulevard. If you enter town on Highway 15, you can join Olas Altas by turning right (west) at the first major intersection.

Waterbirds predominate to a considerable degree, since there are few remaining undisturbed inland habitats near town. The lagoons lining Olas Altas are thick with wintering grebes, cormorants, herons, egrets, ibis, ducks, shorebirds and terns, but they do dry up considerably in the spring and may be filled in sometime in the future. Look for surfbirds in migration on rocky areas such as those near the rotary intersection of Olas Altas and the road leading to Route 15.

Northwest on Olas Altas are more big hotels and a paved road encircling a large lagoon, where Collared Plovers breed in late spring. Beyond this lagoon the road gets rougher, and more birds can be seen. Jacanas may be found in some low grass shallows on the right (west) side of the road. When you reach a final group of restaurants, turn right (west) to reach several spots where you can stop to scan the vast mangrove ponds. The beach north of this area is nice for a lonely stroll.

*　*　*

Mazatlán is the best place to take a short boat trip to see boobies. The bird rocks here, called "Dos Hermanos," are easily seen from the shore. On your way out to sea check for Peregrine Falcons near the cliffs below the lofty lighthouse. As your boat circles the islands you will see a thousand Blue-footed Boobies and several thousand Brown Boobies. Brown Pelicans and Magnificent Frigatebirds are always present. In the winter months look for Arctic Loons, Eared Grebes, Red-billed Tropicbirds (rare), Double-crested Cormorants, Brandt's Cormorants (on the smaller island facing the city), Western Gulls, and Gray-breasted Martins. Nearby islands are covered with tame sea lions that can be easily photographed.

Manx Shearwaters, Northern Phalaropes, and Xantus' Murrelets may be seen on winter boat trips beyond the booby rocks. The La Paz ferry trip provides additional pelagic bird watching.

Birds of Mazatlán

Arctic Loon   R*
Eared Grebe   C*
Least Grebe   A   (*lagoons*)
Western Grebe   R*
Pied-billed Grebe   C*
Manx Shearwater   R   (*offshore*)
Red-billed Tropicbird   R
White Pelican   C*   (*in the vast mangroves at the north end of town*)
Brown Pelican   A
Blue-footed Booby   A   (*over ocean*)
Brown Booby   A   (*over ocean*)
Double-crested Cormorant   A*
Olivaceous Cormorant   A
Brandt's Cormorant   O*
Magnificent Frigatebird   A
Great Blue Heron   A
Green Heron   C*
Little Blue Heron   A
Cattle Egret   C   (*north side*)
Reddish Egret   C
Common Egret   A
Snowy Egret   A
Louisiana Heron   A
Black-crowned Night Heron   R
Yellow-crowned Night Heron   O
White-faced Ibis   A
White Ibis   A
Roseate Spoonbill   O
Fulvous Tree Duck   R
Gadwall   C*
Pintail   A*
Green-winged Teal   A*

Blue-winged Teal   C*
Cinnamon Teal   A*
American Widgeon   A*
Shoveler   A*
Redhead   C*
Ring-necked Duck   R*
Canvasback   C*
Lesser Scaup   A*
Ruddy Duck   A*
Red-breasted Merganser   R*
Turkey Vulture   A
Black Vulture   A
Short-tailed Hawk   R   (*April record*)
Black Hawk   C   (*north side*)
Osprey   C
Caracara   O
Common Gallinule   R
American Coot   A*
Jacana   C   (*lagoons, north side*)
American Oystercatcher   O
Semipalmated Plover   A*
Snowy Plover   R   (*north beach*)
Collared Plover   O
Wilson's Plover   A
Killdeer   A
Black-bellied Plover   C*
Surfbird   C   (*best in spring*)
Ruddy Turnstone   C*
Common Snipe   C*
Long-billed Curlew   A*
Whimbrel   A*
Spotted Sandpiper   A*
Solitary Sandpiper   R   (*migration*)

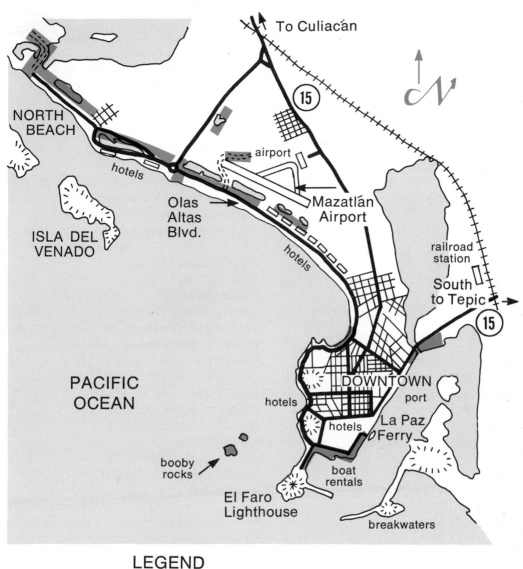

To Culiacán

15

N

NORTH
BEACH

hotels

Olas
Altas
Blvd.

airport

Mazatlán
Airport

ISLA DEL
VENADO

hotels

railroad
station

South
to Tepic

15

PACIFIC
OCEAN

DOWNTOWN

port

hotels

hotels

La Paz
Ferry

booby
rocks

boat
rentals

El Faro
Lighthouse

breakwaters

LEGEND

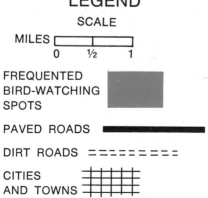

SCALE

MILES

0   ½   1

FREQUENTED
BIRD-WATCHING
SPOTS

PAVED ROADS

DIRT ROADS

CITIES
AND TOWNS

MAZATLÁN, SINALOA

Wandering Tattler   R*   (*April best*)
Willet   A
Greater Yellowlegs   A*
Lesser Yellowlegs   A*
Knot   C   (*migration*)
Least Sandpiper   A*
Dunlin   O*
Short-billed Dowitcher   A*
Long-billed Dowitcher   A*
Stilt Sandpiper   O*
Western Sandpiper   A*
Marbled Godwit   A*
Sanderling   A*
American Avocet   A*
Black-necked Stilt   A
Wilson's Phalarope   A   (*late April and late summer*)
Northern Phalarope   C*   (*offshore*)
Western Gull   C*
Herring Gull   C*
California Gull   C*
Ring-billed Gull   A*
Laughing Gull   A
Bonaparte's Gull   C*
Heermann's Gull   C
Gull-billed Tern   A   (*lagoons*)
Forster's Tern   A*
Common Tern   C*
Least Tern   A   (*summer*)
Royal Tern   A
Elegant Tern   C
Caspian Tern   A
Black Tern   A   (*autumn*)
Black Skimmer   C
Xantus' Murrelet   R   (*offshore*)
White-winged Dove   O
Mourning Dove   O
Ground Dove   A
Ruddy Ground Dove   R
Inca Dove   A
White-fronted Dove   R
Groove-billed Ani   C
White-naped Swift   O   (*on north side*)
Cinnamon Hummingbird   R
Broad-billed Hummingbird   A
Belted Kingfisher   A*
Ringed Kingfisher   R   (*north side*)
Amazon Kingfisher   R   (*winter strays*)
(Green)

Green Kingfisher   C   (*north side*)
Gila Woodpecker   A
Golden-cheeked Woodpecker   R   (*in palms*)
Rose-throated Becard   R
Tropical Kingbird   A
Social Flycatcher   A
Kiskadee Flycatcher   A
Vermilion Flycatcher   A
Violet-Green Swallow   C   (*early spring*)
Tree Swallow   C   (*migration*)
Mangrove Swallow   A   (*lagoons*)
Rough-winged Swallow   A
Barn Swallow   C   (*migration*)
Gray-breasted Martin   O
Mexican Crow   A
House Wren   R*
Mockingbird   A
Curve-billed Thrasher   O
Blue-Gray Gnatcatcher   A*
Water Pipit   R*
Golden Vireo   R*
Bell's Vireo   C
Orange-crowned Warbler   A*
Nashville Warbler   C*
Yellow Warbler   C
Audubon's Warbler   A*
MacGillivray's Warbler   C*
Yellowthroat   A
Fan-tailed Warbler   X   (*February 1965*)
Wilson's Warbler   C*
House Sparrow   A
Meadowlark, species   C
Red-winged Blackbird   A
Orchard Oriole   C
Hooded Oriole   C
Scarlet-headed Oriole   A
Bullock's Oriole   C   (*migration*)
Boat-tailed Grackle   A
Brown-headed Cowbird   C*
Bronzed Cowbird   A
Grayish Saltator   R   (*north side*)
Blue Grosbeak   A
Lazuli Bunting   R*
Varied Bunting   C
Painted Bunting   C
House Finch   A
White-collared Seedeater   C

Blue-Black Grassquit   C   (*best in summer*)
Lesser Goldfinch   C
Green-tailed Towhee   C*
Savannah Sparrow   A*
Grasshopper Sparrow   C*

Vesper Sparrow   C*
Lark Sparrow   A*
Clay-colored Sparrow   C*
White-crowned Sparrow   A*
Lincoln's Sparrow   C*

Route 15: Mazatlán to Villa Union

As you leave Mazatlán you will pass a large estuary to the right (south) which often has Reddish Egrets and thick concentrations of shorebirds at low tide. Contrary to popular belief, the country south of Mazatlán becomes drier, at least for the half-hour stretch to Villa Union.

Just before reaching the Rio del Presidio you will see several ponds covered with lily pads and water hyacinths (except in late spring). These ponds are good for Least Grebes and Jacanas and often have White-faced Ibis, occasional Roseate Spoonbills and Wood Ibis, and Solitary Sandpipers in migration.

After crossing the river you will enter the little town of Villa Union. Route 40, the new paved highway over the Sierra Madres to Durango and Texas, branches east just outside of town.

Route 40: the Durango Highway

Route 40 is the only paved road which crosses the high Sierra Madre Occidental between Arizona and Guadalajara. By far the best bird watching on this road is in Sinaloa, and the trip on into Durango is not really worthwhile. There are no hotel facilities in the mountains, and you will have to camp out if you want to stay overnight.

It might be best to base your trip in Mazatlán. Get up and leave before dawn, taking your lunch with you. It is a two or three hour drive to kilometer post 1164, a good place to be in the morning when the birds are most active. You can return to Mazatlán in the afternoon.

As you leave the southern edge of Villa Union, you will pass through the thorn-scrub and thorn forest of southern Sinaloa. Among the roadside birds here are Short-tailed Hawks, Caracaras, White-fronted Parrots, Lesser Roadrunners, Cinnamon Hummingbirds, Magpie-Jays, Yellow-winged Caciques and Scarlet-headed Orioles. The relative abundance of Military Macaws in the river valley above the town of Concordia is fairly notable, although they may be hard to find in the foliage of the streamside trees. Locate them by their raucous calls.

As you continue rising in elevation, you will get occasional glimpses of the western face of the Sierra Madre Occidental. The ribbon of the highway can be seen wandering off to the northeast. To those who are familiar with the mountain systems of the western United States and Canada, these mountains will appear subdued. With the exception of the cliff faces, they are heavily covered with vegetation. This is due to a lack of frost action and a great amount of chemical weathering caused by high mean temperatures.

As you pass by the villages of Copala and Santa Lucia you may find Short-tailed Hawks, White-fronted Doves, Orange-fronted Parakeets, Lilac-crowned Parrots, huge flocks of White-naped Swifts, Violet-Green Swallows, Gray-breasted Martins, Common Ravens, Blue Mockingbirds, West-

Streaked-backed.   *Mex. Cacique.*

ern Bluebirds, migrant Western Tanagers, Blue Grosbeaks and Black-headed Siskins. Already you should notice a mixing of tropical and highland plants and birds.

Kilometer post 1180 is located in good pine-oak country at 7,500 feet elevation. There are several places to park around the post. In this country you should be able to find Sharp-shinned Hawks, Red-tailed Hawks, Band-tailed Pigeons, Lilac-crowned Parrots, White-eared Hummingbirds, Acorn Woodpeckers, Robins, Brown-backed Solitaires, migrant Warbling Vireos, migrant MacGillivray's Warblers, Western Tanagers, Hepatic Tanagers, Rusty Sparrows, and Chipping Sparrows.

Poorte Parrot

* * *

Kilometer post 1164 marks a high point in Mexican bird watching. It is located about half a mile from El Palmito, Sinaloa (which has a gas station). Down the road a few turns is the Durango state line. Before you begin bird watching here you will need to digest some preliminary information about the country, for the area can be very deceptive. Without care the best birds can be easily missed, and in fact have been missed by number of eminent ornithologists.

You are on the western edge of the Sierras, the meeting place of two great avifaunas—the Sierra Madrean nearctic birds and the west coast neotropicals. The neotropical birds occupy the stream valley and the sides of the steep barrancas (canyons), while the nearctic birds live in the pines and oaks on the flat-topped ridges.

Living between these two extremes in the isolated, higher, humid canyons is one of the most amazing aggregations of plants in Mexico. Here you will see the most northwestern Sacred Fir (*Abies religiosa*) in Mexico, as well as members of the following genera: *Magnolia, Gentiana, Viola, Tillandsia,* and various arboreal orchids.

A small group of rare birds are almost restricted to this unusual ecological niche in west Mexico, the most famous being the large and handsome Tufted Jay, whose closest relatives live in the Andes of South America. The Eared Trogon, Gray-crowned Woodpecker, Hooded Grosbeak, and the northernmost variety of the Green-striped Brush-Finch are likewise localized in the rims of these barrancas.

The Mexican forest fire service maintains a small fire camp called Rancho Liebre Barranca near kilometer post 1164. Just before reaching it you will pass several large billboards picturing the damage done by fires. The camp is a long white building with a large sign in Spanish describing its function. You can park in front of it and get oriented.

The dirt and stone road that winds up the hill behind the camp leads to the barranca. It passes through a forest of pines and oaks dotted with areas of scrub oak and occasional fields. High clearance vehicles may be driven part way up. If you do not have such a vehicle, walk the entire distance.

After about a mile you will find that the road runs into an open area, then makes a major switchback and continues up the hill to the fire tower. Leave the road here and take the well-worn trail past a little enclosed orchard and through some tall pines to the edge of the barranca.

On the road and trail you will see many species. In the brushy areas expect to find White-eared Hummingbirds, Black-eared Bushtits, Brown-throated Wrens, Blue Mockingbirds, Orange-billed Nightingale-Thrushes, Hutton's Vireos, Rufous-capped Warblers, Rufous-capped Brush-Finches, and Rufous-sided Towhees. In the trees, look for Mountain Trogons, Acorn Woodpeckers, Arizona Woodpeckers, Mexican Chickadees, migrant warblers such as Hermit, Townsend's and Audubon's, resident warblers such as Grace's and Red-faced, and numerous Slate-throated Redstarts, Hepatic and other tanagers, Pine Siskins, and Black-headed Siskins. Overhead you may see Lilac-crowned Parrots, flocks of Violet-Green Swallows, and, if you are fortunate, Thick-billed Parrots and Green Parakeets. The only

HUMMINGBIRDS, COTINGAS, FLYCATCHERS

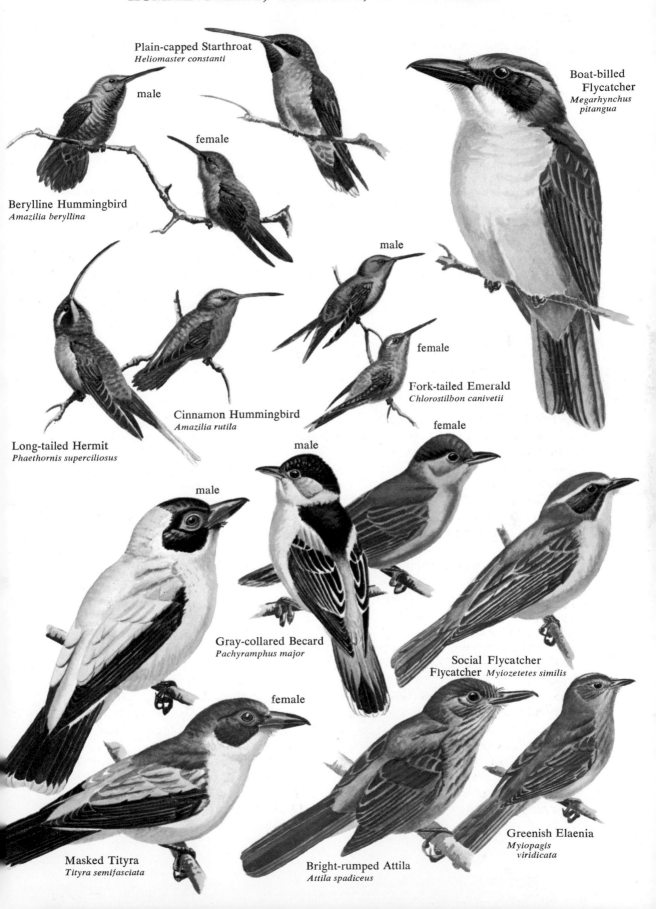

Plain-capped Starthroat
Heliomaster constanti

male

female

Boat-billed
Flycatcher
*Megarhynchus
pitangua*

Berylline Hummingbird
Amazilia beryllina

male

female

Fork-tailed Emerald
Chlorostilbon canivetii

Long-tailed Hermit
Phaethornis superciliosus

Cinnamon Hummingbird
Amazilia rutila

male

female

male

female

Gray-collared Becard
Pachyramphus major

Social Flycatcher
Flycatcher *Myiozetetes similis*

female

Masked Tityra
Tityra semifasciata

Bright-rumped Attila
Attila spadiceus

Greenish Elaenia
*Myiopagis
viridicata*

place you might find large Striped Sparrows is in the tall clumps of bunchgrass about half way up the road on the left (west). A trickling stream in the valley on your right (east) is usually a good place to look for birds, particularly the Red Warbler in winter.

At the edge of the barranca you will find an exposed rock. Sit quietly here, enjoying the magnificent forests below. Watch for the flashing white, blue, and black patterns of the rare Tufted Jay. If you do not see this bird, attract it by giving imitations of the call of a large owl. Our groups have brought out several Tufted Jays with this trick, as well as Green Jays and Steller's Jays.

Near the rock you will find a major trail which descends the left (west) side of the canyon all the way to the bottom, serving a number of scattered ranches. Bird watching on this trail is good, particularly in places where it passes through clumps of large epiphyte-covered oaks.

Another trail goes off to the right (east) through the woods and runs along the top of the rise. After about forty yards it dips down into a tall, moist, broadleaf forest that includes a few specimens of the Sacred Fir. This trail cuts across an old slide area which has a seep running through the middle of it. The seep is bathed in sunlight, and many flowering plants flourish in the moist soil.

You may find up to eight species of humming birds in these flowers. The woods in the area ring with the calls of trogons and the long melodies of Brown-backed Solitaires. When you hear a loud double note repeated every fifteen seconds, you may be on to a Tufted Jay. Also keep an eye out for Golden-browed Warblers and groups of Red-headed Tanagers.

Birds of Kilometer Post 1164, The Durango Highway, and Rancho Liebre Barranca

Note: The bird population varies greatly according to time of year. Many lowland neotropical species fly up to this area after the breeding season. Midwinter can bring cold and snow, causing many species to retreat down the mountain. Remember that a number of the birds of the list occur only in the barranca and are not seen near the main road. Birds definitely known to breed in the area are followed by the symbol (b) on the list.

Turkey Vulture   C
Black Vulture   O
Sharp-shinned Hawk   O
Crested Guan   R   (*barranca*)
Rufous-bellied Chachalaca   R   (*barranca*)
Harlequin Quail   (b)   R
Common Snipe   R*
Band-tailed Pigeon   C   (*barranca best*)
Mourning Dove   R
Ground Dove   R
Inca Dove   R
White-fronted Dove   R
Military Macaw   (b)   R
Green Parakeet   R
Thick-billed Parrot   R
Lilac-crowned Parrot   (b)   O
Whiskered Owl   (b)   R
Flammulated Owl   (b)   R
Least Pygmy Owl   (b)   R

Spotted Owl   R
Stygian Owl   R
Whip-poor-will   (b)   O
White-naped Swift   R
Black Swift   R
Vaux's Swift   R
White-throated Swift   O
Lucifer Hummingbird   R
Black-chinned Hummingbird   R
Broad-tailed Hummingbird   R
Rufous Hummingbird
Calliope Hummingbird   R*
Heloise's Hummingbird   O   *Bumblebee H*
Rivoli's Hummingbird   C
Blue-throated Hummingbird   (b)   O
White-eared Hummingbird   A
Fork-tailed Emerald   R
Eared Trogon   O   (*barranca*)
Mountain Trogon   (b)   C

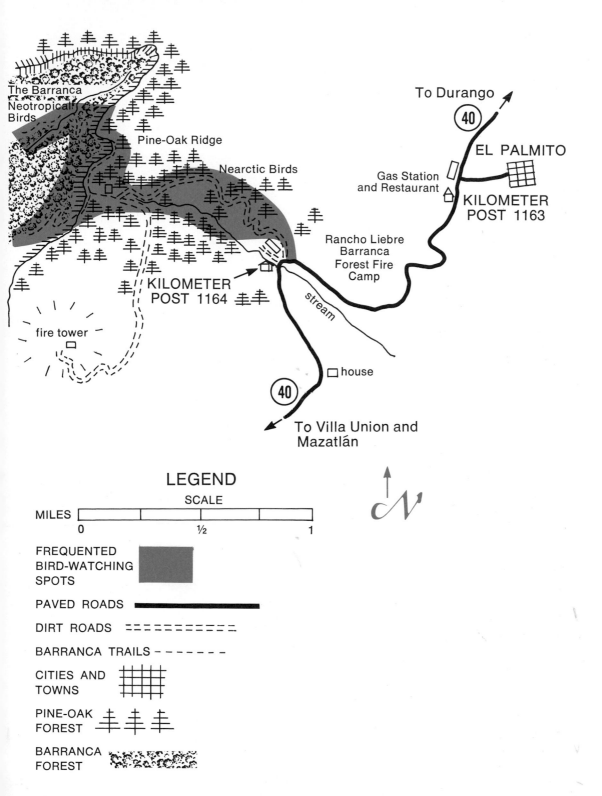

The Barranca
Neotropical
Birds

Pine-Oak Ridge

Nearctic Birds

To Durango

40

EL PALMITO

Gas Station
and Restaurant

KILOMETER
POST 1163

Rancho Liebre
Barranca
Forest Fire
Camp

KILOMETER
POST 1164

stream

fire tower

house

40

To Villa Union and
Mazatlán

LEGEND

SCALE

MILES

0   ½   1

FREQUENTED
BIRD-WATCHING
SPOTS

PAVED ROADS

DIRT ROADS

BARRANCA TRAILS

CITIES AND
TOWNS

PINE-OAK
FOREST

BARRANCA
FOREST

N

Kilometer Post 1164
DURANGO HIGHWAY — EL PALMITO, SINALOA

Coppery-tailed Trogon O
Red-shafted Flicker (b) A
Gray-crowned Woodpecker R (*barranca*)
Acorn Woodpecker (b) C
Hairy Woodpecker O
Arizona Woodpecker (b) C
Ivory-billed Woodcreeper R
White-striped Woodcreeper C (*pines and barranca*)
Bright-rumped Attila R (*barranca*)
Gray-collared Becard R (*barranca*)
Masked Tityra R (*barranca*)
Kiskadee Flycatcher R
Olivaceous Flycatcher C
Hammond's Flycatcher R*
Dusky Flycatcher R*
Gray Flycatcher R*
Pine Flycatcher (b) R
Western Flycatcher (b) O
Coues' Flycatcher O
Western Wood Pewee R
Olive-sided Flycatcher R (*migration*)
Violet-Green Swallow (b) C
Steller's Jay A
Tufted Jay C (*barranca*)
Green Jay R (*barranca*)
Common Raven (b) C
Mexican Crow R
Mexican Chickadee (b) A
Bridled Titmouse C
Black-eared Bushtit (b) A
White-breasted Nuthatch O
Brown Creeper (b) C
Brown-throated Wren (b) A
Spotted Wren R
Blue Mockingbird (b) C
Robin (b) A
White-throated Robin O
Hermit Thrush C
Swainson's Thrush O*
Russet Nightingale Thrush O
Orange-billed Nightingale Thrush O
Western Bluebird O
Brown-backed Solitaire (b) A (*calls often in barranca*)
Ruby-crowned Kinglet A*

Cedar Waxwing O*
Gray Silky Flycatcher (b) C (*erratic*)
Hutton's Vireo A
Solitary Vireo C
Crescent-chested Warbler (b) R
Audubon's Warbler A*
Black-throated Gray Warbler O*
Townsend's Warbler C*
Hermit Warbler C*
Grace's Warbler (b) O
MacGillivray's Warbler C*
Fan-tailed Warbler R (*barranca*)
Red Warbler C (*winters*)
Golden-browed Warbler (b) A (*barranca*)
Rufous-capped Warbler (b) C
Red-faced Warbler O
Wilson's Warbler C*
Slate-throated Redstart (b) A
Scarlet-headed Oriole R
Black-vented Oriole (b) R
Scott's Oriole R
Blue-hooded Euphonia (b) R
Western Tanager O*
Hepatic Tanager (b) A
Summer Tanager R
Flame-colored Tanager (b) O
Red-headed Tanager (b) A (*barranca*)
Yellow Grosbeak R
Black-headed Grosbeak C
Varied Bunting O
Hooded Grosbeak R (*barranca*)
Pine Siskin (b) O
Black-headed Siskin (b) O
Lesser Goldfinch O
Rufous-capped Brush-Finch (b) C (*pine-oak*)
Green-striped Brush-Finch O (*barranca*)
Rufous-sided Towhee (b) A
Striped Sparrow O (*bunch-grass*)
Rusty Sparrow O
Mexican Junco A
Chipping Sparrow A
Lincoln's Sparrow O*

ROUTE 15: VILLA UNION TO SINALOA-NAYARIT STATELINE

HEADING SOUTH on Route 15 once more, you will enter the tropical savanna habitats of the lowlands. These are lightly forested and grassy areas scattered with palms, roadside ponds, and farms. One interesting bird in winter and spring is the White-naped Swift, which may be seen flying in flocks over the fields. The most frequented bird watching localities are near kilometer post 1159 north of Rosario, post 1108 south of Rosario, and post 1084 south of Escuinapa.

After crossing the Rio Baluarte and taking a curve, you will come to a small river bridge. Park on the little dirt road on your right (west) and walk quietly among the tall trees along the river. Iguanas can be seen under the bridge and in the trees. A long pond lined with low trees just to your right (west) attracts many species. Among the birds which have been seen here are Orange-fronted Parakeets, Mangrove Cuckoos, Cinnamon Hummingbirds, Green Kingfishers, Russet-crowned Motmots,

Rose-throated Becards, Social Flycatchers, Kiskadee Flycatchers, Happy Wrens, Rufous-backed Robins, Yellow-Green Vireos, Olive-backed Warblers, Yellow-winged Caciques, Scarlet-headed Orioles, Grayish Saltators, Yellow Grosbeaks, Blue Buntings and White-collared Seedeaters. The area to the right (west) of the pond is gradually being taken over by man, but is still worth a stroll.

About nine miles from the Rio Baluarte, Route 15 passes through the good-sized town of Escuinapa. A poor road goes west through the mangrove swamps which stretch from Escuinapa to Teacapán on the coast. This is as far north as you will find Boat-billed Herons. Route 15 to the Nayarit border passes through more varied tropical habitats, but no dense forests thrive here. Except during the late spring dry season, a multitude of roadside ponds and puddles attract many birds.

Birds Between Mazatlán and the Sinaloa-Nayarit Border

Least Grebe   A   (*in ponds with cover*)
Pied-billed Grebe   C*
White Pelican   C*   (*in flocks on and over coastal mangroves*)
Olivaceous Cormorant   C
Anhinga   R
Great Blue Heron   C
Green Heron   A*
Little Blue Heron   C
Cattle Egret   C   (*Escuinapa area is best*)
Common Egret   A
Snowy Egret   A
Louisiana Heron   A
Wood Ibis   O
White-faced Ibis   A
White Ibis   A
Roseate Spoonbill   R
Black-bellied Tree Duck   R
Gadwall   C*
Pintail   C*

Green-winged Teal   A*
Blue-winged Teal   A*
Cinnamon Teal   C*
American Widgeon   A*
Shoveler   A*
Lesser Scaup   C*
Ruddy Duck   C*
Turkey Vulture   A
Black Vulture   A
Sharp-shinned Hawk   C*
Cooper's Hawk   C*
Red-tailed Hawk   A
Swainson's Hawk   C   (*migration*)
Zone-tailed Hawk   R*
White-tailed Hawk   O
Gray Hawk   A
Harris' Hawk   C
Black Hawk   C
Blackish Crane Hawk   R   (*south of Escuinapa is best*)

Collared Forest-Falcon   R
Caracara   C
Sparrow Hawk   A*
Common Gallinule   C
American Coot   A*
Jacana   A   (*R in late spring*)
Killdeer   A*
Common Snipe   C*
Spotted Sandpiper   A*
Solitary Sandpiper   R   (*migration*)
Willet   C*
Greater Yellowlegs   A*
Lesser Yellowlegs   A*
Least Sandpiper   A*
Western Sandpiper   A*
Dowitcher, species   A*
Marbled Godwit   R*
American Avocet   C*
Black-necked Stilt   A
Red-billed Pigeon   O
White-winged Dove   A
Mourning Dove   C*
Ground Dove   A
Ruddy Ground Dove   C
Inca Dove   A
White-fronted Dove   C
Military Macaw   O   (*flying high*)
Orange-fronted Parakeet   A
Blue-rumped Parrotlet   O
White-fronted Parrot   C
Lilac-crowned Parrot   O
Mangrove Cuckoo   R
Groove-billed Ani   A
Common Potoo   R   (*best seen at night*)
White-naped Swift   A   (*January–April*)
Black Swift   O*
Vaux's Swift   C   (*April migration*)
Plain-capped Star-throat   R
Cinnamon Hummingbird   C
Broad-billed Hummingbird   C
Belted Kingfisher   A*
Ringed Kingfisher   R   (*in roadside ponds*)
Green Kingfisher   C
Russet-crowned Motmot   O
Gila Woodpecker   C
Golden-cheeked Woodpecker   O
Ladder-backed Woodpecker   O
Rose-throated Becard   O

Tropical Kingbird   A
Cassin's Kingbird   C*
Thick-billed Kingbird   A
Social Flycatcher   A
Kiskadee Flycatcher   A
Sulphur-bellied Flycatcher   C   (*summer*)
Olivaceous Flycatcher   C
Black Phoebe   C
Empidonax, species   A
Coues' Flycatcher   O*
Vermilion Flycatcher   A
Tree Swallow   C   (*migration*)
Mangrove Swallow   A   (*over rivers*)
Rough-winged Swallow   A
Barn Swallow   C   (*April migration*)
Cliff Swallow   O   (*migration*)
Purplish-backed   Jay   C   (*on   lightly
     wooded hillsides*)
Magpie-Jay   A
Raven, species   A
Mexican Crow   A
Bar-vented Wren   O
Happy Wren   C
Mockingbird   A
Rufous-backed Robin   O
Blue-Gray Gnatcatcher   A*
Water Pipit   C*
Loggerhead Shrike   A*
Solitary Vireo   C*
Yellow-Green Vireo   O   (*summer*)
Warbling Vireo   C*
Orange-crowned Warbler   A*
Nashville Warbler   C*
Lucy's Warbler   O   (*migration*)
Olive-backed Warbler   C   (*wooded areas*)
Audubon's Warbler   C*
Black-throated Gray Warbler   C*
MacGillivray's Warbler   A*
Yellow-breasted Chat   C
Wilson's Warbler   A*
House Sparrow   A
Yellow-winged Cacique   A
Red-winged Blackbird   C
Orchard Oriole   C
Hooded Oriole   C
Scarlet-headed Oriole   A
Black-vented Oriole   R
Bullock's Oriole   C   (*migration*)

Boat-tailed Grackle   A
Bronzed Cowbird   A
√Grayish Saltator   A   (*in wooded areas*)
Yellow Grosbeak   O
Black-headed Grosbeak   C   (*migration*)
Blue Grosbeak   C
Blue Bunting   R
√ Indigo Bunting   C*
√ Varied Bunting   A
Painted Bunting   C

House Finch   A
White-collared Seedeater   C
Blue-Black Grassquit   C   (*best in summer*)
Lesser Goldfinch   C
Green-tailed Towhee   C*
Lark Sparrow   A*
White-crowned Sparrow   C*
Lincoln's Sparrow   C*

CHAPTER IV

NAYARIT

ROUTE 15: SINALOA-NAYARIT STATELINE TO CRUCERO SAN BLAS

FOUR MILES SOUTH of the Nayarit border lies a set of junctions. A short road runs inland to the nearby town of Acaponeta. Route 15 continues south. On the right, Route 10 turns westward through a rich agricultural area before it reaches the extensive marshes that lie behind the low, sandy barrier coast.

* * *

The Route 10 sidetrip may prove very rewarding. It takes in areas important for wintering northern waterfowl and many resident waders. The road travels the Rio Acaponeta Valley, rich in crops of corn, beans, sugar cane, tobacco, cotton, and tomatoes. A wide variety of habitats, including thorn shrubbery, thorn woodland, sloughs, freshwater ponds, salt-water ponds, grassy brackish open swamps, and mangrove swamps is covered on this route. As the road progresses towards the coast, its surface becomes all-weather gravel which can be quite dusty during the dry season.

The Puerto del Rio tidal channel is located at La Bara, a group of fishing shacks beyond Tecuala. The state of Nayarit maintains a free cable ferry across the estuary to Playa Novilleros, a small town at the edge of a two-mile-wide coastal barrier beach. The beach is forty miles long, and the sand is hard and safe to drive on during low tide. In fact, local buses use the beach as part of their regular routes. The birds are somewhat limited, but include Brown Pelicans, American Oystercatchers, gulls, and terns. Some of these species nest on the upper margin of the beach. Diving ducks are common in the winter. The estuaries and marshes might be checked for Fulvous Tree-Ducks.

During the rains a large rookery is active six miles down the estuary towards the sea. Approximately 1,200 nests were counted here during the dry season. To visit the rookery you will have to hire a canoa, motor, and boatman. The cost will be about 125 pesos for a four-hour trip.

The areas most frequented by a number of rare birds are the low thorny forests that have developed on the sandy-saline soils behind the beaches. Such coastal forests have a comparatively limited number of breeding species but are very popular stop-over places for northern migrants and down-slope wanderers in the winter.

These woods are the only places in Mexico where Rose-breasted Thrush-Tanagers can be found with any regularity. In December you can see up to twenty in two days. In July 1966 a nest was found with three half-grown young. On the same trip, the nest and young of a Mangrove Cuckoo was found in one of these dry thorny forests more than a mile from the nearest mangrove trees. In the

PARROTS, MOTMOT, TROGON

Citreoline Trogon
Trogon citreolus

Russet-crowned Motmot
Momotus mexicanus

Military Macaw
Ara militaris

Lilac-crowned Parrot
Amazona finschi

Orange-fronted Parakeet
Aratinga canicularis

Green Parakeet
Aratinga holochlora

White-fronted Parrot
Amazona albifrons

Blue-rumped Parrotlet
Forpus cyanopygius

heavier forest, Blackish Crane-Hawks can be found with fair regularity. When flushed, this scarlet-eyed hawk generally flies less than fifty yards before resettling. Most often the best views can be had by carefully stalking resettled birds.

Before you explore these areas, be sure to take precautions against ticks and chiggers in the drier seasons and midges and mosquitoes in the wet season.

* * *

Back on Route 15 South, you will soon come to a bright orange steel bridge over the Rio Acaponeta. Beyond here, at kilometer post 1030, you will see a pond to the east. Cattle Egrets and Jacanas, as well as the waterbirds that appear in the bird list below can often be seen here.

Beyond the bridge the country becomes wooded in patches. Stretches of typical savanna country with low fan palms dotting coarse grasslands make up the rest of the landscape. Note how strangler figs have enveloped some of the palms.

Between kilometer posts 996 and 995 some year-round ponds have breeding Jacanas, as well as groups of ibis and other waterbirds. The watery vegetation is a good place for Ground Chat. Keep an eye open for Bare-throated Tiger Herons that sulk in the shadows near kilometer post 991.

About an hour south of Acaponeta you will cross the Rio San Pedro. On the other side lies a junction with a big gasoline station and many small shops selling native wares, fruits, and dried bananas. Occasion-

ally you will meet bird vendors peddling Orange-fronted Parakeets, Blue-rumped Parrotlets, Brown-backed Solitaires, and buntings (Varied, Indigo, and Painted). The small city of Tuxpan lies five miles to your right (west) in agricultural country.

* * *

Nine miles on, Route 32 branches west off Route 15 to the city of Santiago Ixcuintla. A mile down this road, on the left (south) side, lies a pond which often hosts many Wood Ibis. Beyond Santiago, Route 32 continues towards the coast through twenty miles of fields of tobacco, corn, beans, chiles, tomatoes, cotton, palm-oil nuts, bananas, and pineapples. Elegant Quail, Bar-vented Wrens, and Blue-Black Grassquits live in the weeds.

The road becomes a poor dirt track as you approach a small section of mangroves. Turn right (north) at the junction here and go on for two miles to Boca de Camichin, a fine beach locality. This road is similar to the Playa Novilleros road.

* * *

Continuing south on Route 15 you will soon cross the Rio Grande de Santiago, the longest river in Mexico. Its waters cut deep barrancas before spreading over the coastal mangroves of Nayarit. The highway will take you through good savanna habitats until you arrive at Crucero San Blas, where truckers go straight and bird watchers turn west.

Birds Between Sinaloa-Nayarit Border and Crucero San Blas

Note: This bird list does not include the side road Route 10.

Least Grebe	A	Cattle Egret	C
Pied-billed Grebe	R*	Common Egret	A
Olivaceous Cormorant	A	Snowy Egret	A
Anhinga	O	Louisiana Heron	A
Great Blue Heron	C	Bare-throated Tiger Heron	O
Green Heron	C*	Wood Ibis	C
Little Blue Heron	C	White-faced Ibis	C

White Ibis   C
Roseate Spoonbill   C
Gadwall   C*
Pintail   C*
Green-winged Teal   C*
Blue-winged Teal   C*
Cinnamon Teal   C*
American Widgeon   C*
Shoveler   C*
Turkey Vulture   A
Black Vulture   A
Sharp-shinned Hawk   C*
Cooper's Hawk   C*
Red-tailed Hawk   C
Swainson's Hawk   C   (*migration*)
Zone-tailed Hawk   O*
Short-tailed Hawk   O
White-tailed Hawk   O
Gray Hawk   C
Black Hawk   C
Caracara   C
Sparrow Hawk   C*
Elegant Quail   O
Common Gallinule   C
American Coot   A*
Jacana   A
Killdeer   A
Spotted Sandpiper   C*
Greater Yellowlegs   C*
Lesser Yellowlegs   C*
Least Sandpiper   C*
Dowitcher, species   C*
American Avocet   C*
Black-necked Stilt   A
Red-billed Pigeon   C
White-winged Dove   A
Mourning Dove   C*
Ground Dove   A
Ruddy Ground Dove   C
Inca Dove   A
White-fronted Dove   C
Military Macaw   O   (*flying high*)
Orange-fronted Parakeet   A
Blue-rumped Parrotlet   C
White-fronted Parrot   A
Lilac-crowned Parrot   C
Squirrel Cuckoo   O
Groove-billed Ani   A

White-naped Swift   C   (*January–April*)
Black Swift   R*
Plain-capped Star-throat   C
Cinnamon Hummingbird   C
Broad-billed Hummingbird   C
Belted Kingfisher   A*
Ringed Kingfisher   R
Amazon Kingfisher   R   (*by wooded streams*)
Green Kingfisher   C
Russet-crowned Motmot   R
Gila Woodpecker   C
Golden-cheeked Woodpecker   A   (Flint-billed)
Pale-billed Woodpecker   O
Rose-throated Becard   R
Masked Tityra   O
Tropical Kingbird   A
Western Kingbird   R*
Thick-billed Kingbird   A
Scissor-tailed   Flycatcher   X   (*December 1962*)
Boat-billed Flycatcher   R
Social Flycatcher   A
Kiskadee Flycatcher   A
Vermilion Flycatcher   C*
Mangrove Swallow   C
Rough-winged Swallow   A
San Blas Jay   R
Purplish-backed Jay   C   (Beechey's Jay)
Magpie-Jay   A
Mexican Crow   A
Common Raven   C
House Wren   O*
Bar-vented Wren   O
Happy Wren   O
Long-billed Marsh Wren   C*
Mockingbird   A
Rufous-backed Robin   O
Hermit Thrush   (R*)
Blue-Gray Gnatcatcher   A*
White-lored Gnatcatcher   R
Water Pipit   C*
Loggerhead Shrike   A*
Orange-crowned Warbler   A*
Nashville Warbler   C*
Olive-backed Warbler   R
Audubon's Warbler   C*
MacGillivray's Warbler   C*

Ground Chat   O
Wilson's Warbler   C*
House Sparrow   A
Yellow-winged Cacique   A
Meadowlark, species   C
Red-winged Blackbird   C
Orchard Oriole   C
Scarlet-headed Oriole   A
Black-vented Oriole   R
Bronzed Cowbird   A
Boat-tailed Grackle   A

Grayish Saltator   C
Yellow Grosbeak   O
Blue Grosbeak   C*
Indigo Bunting
Varied Bunting   A
Painted Bunting   C
White-collared Seedeater   C
Blue-Black Grassquit   A   (*O in winter*)
Vesper Sparrow   C*
Lark Sparrow   C*
Lincoln's Sparrow   C*

ROUTE 54: CRUCERO SAN BLAS TO SAN BLAS

NAYARIT ROUTE 54 west from Crucero San Blas takes you into the richest bird watching area in west Mexico. This route is about twenty-three miles long and is much less traveled than Route 15. Since it was paved in the mid-1950's, it has brought the inevitable influx of population and concurrent disturbance of natural habitat. The area is still good for bird watching, however.

Immediately after you turn onto Route 54, check the pond on your left (south) for waders and ducks. Ring-necked Ducks can be seen here in the winter. Numerous finches flutter through the tilled fields. Elegant Quail, Groove-billed Anis, and Lesser Roadrunners may be seen on or near the road.

In the uncultivated areas you will find remnants of savanna, thorn forest, and deciduous forest. You will do well to check as many weedy, grassy, and brushy areas as you can, keeping an eye open for Orchard Orioles, Yellow Grosbeaks, Blue Grosbeaks, Blue Buntings, Indigo Buntings, Varied Buntings, Dickcissels, White-collared Seedeaters, Ruddy-breasted Seedeaters, Blue-

Black Grassquits, Lesser Goldfinches, Grasshopper Sparrows, and Stripe-headed Sparrows.

Hummingbirds may be quite common in lush growths of roadside flowers or on low telephone wire perches. Peak numbers are in October; lowest are in spring. This is the best area for the Fork-tailed Emerald. Other species to look for are Black-chinned, Violet-crowned, Berylline, Broad-billed, and Cinnamon Hummingbirds and Plain-capped Star-throats.

If you drive this road at dawn or dusk, you may witness impressive flights of White-fronted Parrots, lesser numbers of Lilac-crowned Parrots and Orange-fronted Parakeets, and an occasional group of Military Macaws.

At the top of a hill above the little town of Singaita you will pass suddenly and quietly into thick jungle. It is wisest to pass through this fascinating area and drive straight on into San Blas to obtain accomodations. Later you can return to do some jungle bird watching.

THE TOWN OF SAN BLAS

SAN BLAS is a small fishing village. In recent years it has attracted more and more bird watchers, naturalists, and tourists, but the modern, glittering accommodations of

Acapulco and Mazatlán have not yet been built here. The cobblestone streets are lined with palms, and graceful coconut palms line the beaches. Ruins of a once-important

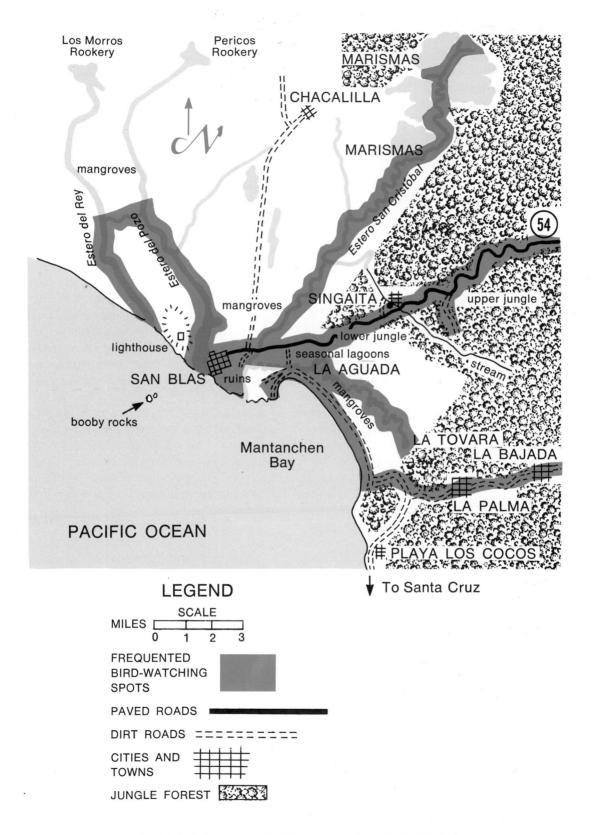

Los Morros
Rookery

Pericos
Rookery

MARISMAS

CHACALILLA

mangroves

MARISMAS

Estero del Rey

Estero del Pozo

Estero San Cristobal

mangroves

SINGAITA

upper jungle

lower jungle

lighthouse

seasonal lagoons

stream

SAN BLAS

ruins

LA AGUADA

booby rocks

mangroves

LA TOVARA

LA BAJADA

Mantanchen
Bay

LA PALMA

PACIFIC OCEAN

PLAYA LOS COCOS

To Santa Cruz

54

LEGEND

SCALE

MILES

0   1   2   3

FREQUENTED
BIRD-WATCHING
SPOTS

PAVED ROADS

DIRT ROADS

CITIES AND
TOWNS

JUNGLE FOREST

SAN BLAS, NAYARIT and ENVIRONS

Spanish port city, including a huge fort and an impressive cathedral, are perched on a high cliff overlooking the present-day town and the ocean. You may want to take the steep cobblestone road up to this point to scan the area and gain orientation. Look for Orange-fronted Parakeets, Squirrel Cuckoos, Barn Owls (roosting in the cathedral), Fork-tailed Emeralds, Citreoline Trogons, Russet-crowned Motmots, Bright-rumped Attilas, Gray-breasted Martins, Rufous-backed Robins, wintering Orange-billed Nightingale-Thrushes, American Redstarts, Yellow-winged Caciques, and Grayish Saltators.

San Blas borders several types of bird habitats. It lies at the southern edge of the great mangrove swamps, at the northern edge of a transitional tropical deciduous forest, and at the northwestern edge of the high central volcanic cordillera. An estuary fills with tidal waters, and a white sand beach stretches out to the south. Coconut plantations with tall trees, grass, and bushes occupy much of the land around the town.

A good variety of water and jungle birds can be seen in the immediate area, as the bird lists show. Finding them will be an exciting experience if the basic precautions of tropical bird watching discussed on page 7 are observed.

San Blas and its environs are especially good for seeing large populations of parrots. You can find them easily if you know how. Parrots are best seen in the early morning or late afternoon hours when they are noisily flying in groups to or from their roosting and feeding locations. During midday they usually occur singly, feeding quietly in fruiting trees where they are almost indistinguishable from the foliage.

The most common parrot around San Blas is the small Orange-fronted Parakeet, easily recognized by its long pointed tail. One of its favorite roosting places is a grove of tall coconut palms and mangroves along the trail to the airstrip (see Map 14). In the early morning and late afternoon flocks can be seen flying over the Hotel Bucanero and the old customs house. Up near the ruins of the fort and the cathedral, flocks fly extremely low. In the morning, look for these birds overhead on all the trails on the outskirts of town.

Of the larger parrot varieties, White-fronted Parrots are by far the most common around San Blas. They are much heavier than the parakeets and have a short, almost square tail. They are fairly common in the mangroves and very common in the Singaita jungle where noisy flocks fly overhead at dawn and dusk. On boat trips in the mangroves and walks along the road in the Singaita jungle you should be able to find these parrots feeding in the treetops. A few usually can be seen around the ruins and the base of the cliff trail near town. Notice how they use their beaks when climbing along tree limbs.

Lilac-crowned Parrots are quite sporadic around San Blas, generally preferring higher elevations. You will probably see them only in the jungle near Singaita. Although larger than the White-fronted Parrot, the Lilac-crown can be quite hard to distinguish from a distance.

The tiny Blue-rumped Parrotlet is only five inches long. Flocks numbering up to one hundred birds will fly overhead like hoards of locusts, then disappear into the tops of fruiting trees where their size and coloring make them indistinguishable from the leaves. Look for these little birds in areas with scattered trees both in town and around the jungle. A characteristic soft chattering in flight should direct your attention to a flock.

In the winter a few Military Macaws occasionally come down to the San Blas area from the mountains. You may see them flying by the village of Singaita or over the mangroves early in the morning. These magnificent birds are much larger than the common parrots of San Blas. Recognize them by their extraordinarily long tails.

SWALLOW, JAYS, WRENS, ROBINS

Tufted Jay
Cyanocorax dickeyi

Purplish-backed Jay
Cissilopha beechei

Bar-vented Wren
Thryothorus sinaloa

White-throated Robin
Turdus assimilis

Happy Wren
Thryothorus felix

Magpie Jay
Calocitta formosa

Blue Mockingbird
Melanotis caerulescens

Mangrove Swallow
Tachycineta albilinea

Spotted Wren
Campylorhynchus jocosus

Rufous-backed Robin
Turdus rufopalliatus

San Blas Jay
Cissilopha sanblasiana

The San Blas Outskirts: Trails and Boat Trips Near the Town

SEVERAL TRAILS near the town of San Blas are good for bird watching strolls. Use the little zocolo, or main plaza, as a point of reference. San Blas is laid out in a grid pattern, with streets running at right angles. Route 54 (known as Calle Juarez) runs northeast towards the ruins, the Estero San Cristobal Bridge, and Tepic. Calle Juarez heads southwest from the zocolo towards the Hotel Bucanero and the estuary known as the Estero del Pozo. Calle H. Batallon de San Blas intersects the zocolo and Calle Juarez. It runs southeast to reach the major swimming beach and the Hotel Playa Hermosa and travels northwest to the tiny airstrip of San Blas. Walks in all directions are worthwhile.

Walk to the southeast during the early morning hours. Many Orange-fronted Parakeets can be seen on the wing. Scarlet-headed and Hooded Orioles play in the numerous coconut palms. In the summer, Blue-Black Grassquits, White-collared Seedeaters, and migrant flocks of Blue Grosbeaks may be seen in numbers. Watch for a little Ferruginous Owl perched over the road on the branches of a broad-leafed tree. If you find one of these birds stay to watch it, for many other species will probably stop to bother it. Over the water near the Playa Hermosa Hotel you may find hundreds of Magnificent Frigatebirds.

Take Calle H. Batallon de San Blas northwest beyond the church. Turn left when you reach the airstrip. Here you will encounter a maze of trails through the heavy underbrush under the coconut palms. Look for Ruddy Ground Doves, huge flocks of Orange-fronted Parakeets (roosting in the trees at night), Cinnamon Hummingbirds, Russet-crowned Motmots, Linneated Woodpeckers, Golden-cheeked Woodpeckers, Rose-throated Becards, Flammulated Flycatchers, Bar-vented Wrens, Happy Wrens, Blue Mockingbirds, Rufous-backed Robins, Scarlet-headed Orioles, Rose-breasted Thrush-Tanagers, Grayish Saltators, and Painted Buntings.

Another good trail can be reached by taking Calle H. Batallon de San Blas three blocks southeast from the zocolo, then turning left (northeast) on the first dirt road spur. This road heads directly to the foot of the cliff of the ruins of old San Blas. As you walk toward the base of the cliff below, carefully look for a colony of Stripe-headed Sparrows in the heavy weeds and bushes on your right.

The road veers right (southeast) near the cliff and passes through some fine flat bird watching country covered with heavy shrubbery, tall trees, and broad meadows. The trail ends at the Estero San Cristobal. Birds to look for include Elegant Quail, Ruddy Ground Doves, White-fronted Doves, Orange-fronted Parakeets, Blue-rumped Parrotlets, Ferruginous Owls, Cinnamon Hummingbirds, Coppery-tailed Trogons, Russet-crowned Motmots, Happy Wrens, Blue Mockingbirds, wintering Orange-billed Nightingale-Thrushes, Rufous-backed Robins, many wintering warblers, Yellow-winged Caciques, orioles, buntings, grosbeaks, White-collared Seedeaters, and Blue-Black Grassquits.

Two boat trips leave from a dock near the old customs house in San Blas. First, a dugout canoe regularly crosses the Estero del Pozo. The boat will land you on the shores of a peninsula with a lighthouse. Old walls and cannons date back to Spanish occupation. The inland beach to your right (north) on the river is packed with shorebirds at certain tides. Birds of particular interest here are wintering Wandering Tattlers and Knots. The seaward beach on the left (south) ends at a point, a favorite resting place for shorebirds, gulls, terns, and Black Skimmers.

Another excellent boat trip goes up the Estero del Rey. In the winter the estuary shores are crowded with waterbirds. Get your boatman to go as close to the banks as possible. Underneath the aerial roots of the mangroves you may catch a glimpse of the colorful and elusive Rufous-necked Wood Rail. Ringed, Belted, and Green Kingfishers are quite common. Farther up the estuary you can see the region's chief colony of Roseate Spoonbills in the late summer. Keep a lookout for Boat-billed Herons and White Pelicans.

Birds of San Blas I: The Town, the Ruins, and the Estuaries

Brown Pelican   A
Blue-footed Booby   A   (*over the ocean*)
White Pelican   R   (*soaring high*)
Brown Booby   C   (*over the ocean*)
Double-crested Cormorant   C*
Olivaceous Cormorant   A
Magnificent Frigatebird   A
Great Blue Heron   C
Green Heron   C*
Little Blue Heron   A
Reddish Egret   O
Common Egret   A
Snowy Egret   A
Louisiana Heron   A
Yellow-crowned Night Heron   O
Boat-billed Heron   R
Wood Ibis   O   (*soaring high*)
White-faced Ibis   R
White Ibis   A
Roseate Spoonbill   O   (*soaring high*)
Shoveler   O*
Lesser Scaup   C*
Black Vulture   A
Turkey Vulture   A
Zone-tailed Hawk   R*
Gray Hawk   O
Black Hawk   O
Blackish Crane Hawk   R
Osprey   A
Caracara   O
Sparrow Hawk   C*
Elegant Quail   O   (*near Playa Hermosa Hotel*)
Rufous-necked Wood Rail   R
Common Gallinule   O
American Coot   C*
Semipalmated Plover   A*

Snowy Plover   R*
Collared Plover   O
Wilson's Plover   A
Killdeer   O
Black-bellied Plover   A*
Surfbird   R   (*on rocks in estuary*)
Ruddy Turnstone   A*
Long-billed Curlew   A*
Whimbrel   A*
Spotted Sandpiper   A*
Wandering Tattler   R*
Willet   A*
Greater Yellowlegs   A*
Lesser Yellowlegs   A*
Knot   O*
Least Sandpiper   A*
Dunlin   O*
Dowitcher, species   A*
Western Sandpiper   A*
Marbled Godwit   A*
Sanderling   A*
Black-necked Stilt   C
Glaucous-winged   Gull   X   (*December 1964*)
Western Gull   C*
Herring Gull   C*
California Gull   O*
Ring-billed Gull   A*
Laughing Gull   C
Heermann's Gull   C
Gull-billed Tern   O
Forster's Tern   A*
Common Tern   A*
Least Tern   A   (*summer*)
Royal Tern   A
Elegant Tern   C   (*over the ocean*)
Caspian Tern   A

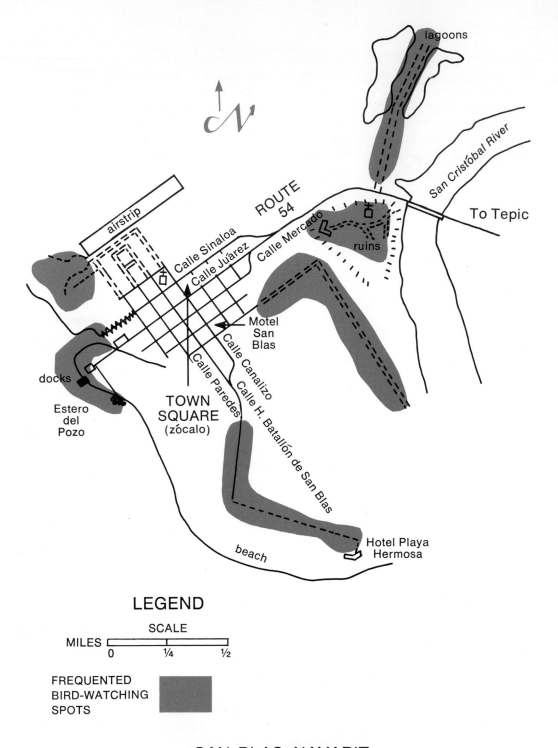

lagoons

San Cristóbal River

ROUTE 54

To Tepic

airstrip

Calle Sinaloa

Calle Juárez

Calle Mercado

ruins

Motel San Blas

docks

Calle Paredes

Calle Canalizo

Calle H. Batallón de San Blas

Estero del Pozo

TOWN SQUARE (zócalo)

beach

Hotel Playa Hermosa

LEGEND

SCALE

MILES

0   ¼   ½

FREQUENTED
BIRD-WATCHING
SPOTS

SAN BLAS, NAYARIT
Town and Outskirts

Black Skimmer   A   (*Flocks roost on sand bars at low tide.*)

Red-billed Pigeon   C

White-winged Dove   A

Ground Dove   A

Ruddy Ground Dove   A   (*best seen on north side near airstrip*)

White-fronted Dove   C   (*near ruins*)

Orange-fronted Parakeet   A   (*in palms and on evening flights over the ruins*)

Blue-rumped Parrotlet   C   (*near ruins*)

White-fronted Parrot   A   (*flying over town and near ruins*)

Squirrel Cuckoo   R   (*near ruins*)

Groove-billed Ani   A

Barn Owl   R   (*in cathedral*)

Ferruginous Owl   O   (*chiefly at dusk*)

Common Nighthawk   C   (*flying over town*)

Lesser Nighthawk   O   (*flying over town*)

Vaux's Swift   C*   (*flying over town*)

Black-chinned Hummingbird   R*

Plain-capped Star-throat   R

Berylline Hummingbird   R   (*near ruins*)

Cinnamon Hummingbird   A

Fork-tailed Emerald   O   (*near ruins*)

Broad-billed Hummingbird   C

Citreoline Trogon   C   (*near ruins*)

Coppery-tailed Trogon   O

Belted Kingfisher   C*

Ringed Kingfisher   O

Green Kingfisher   O

Russet-crowned Motmot   O   (*near ruins*)

Linneated Woodpecker   R

Golden-cheeked Woodpecker   A

Pale-billed Woodpecker   R

Bright-rumped Attila   R   (*near ruins*)

Rose-throated Becard   O   (*near ruins*)

Masked Tityra   O   (*near ruins*)

Tropical Kingbird   A

Thick-billed Kingbird   C   (*near ruins*)

Boat-billed Flycatcher   O   (*near ruins*)

Social Flycatcher   A

Kiskadee Flycatcher   A

Olivaceous Flycatcher   O*

Flammulated Flycatcher   R

Empidonax, light-breasted   R*

Western Flycatcher   O*

Coues' Flycatcher   O*

Olive-sided Flycatcher   R   (*October migration*)

Vermilion Flycatcher   C*

Mangrove Swallow   A

Bank Swallow   R*

Rough-winged Swallow   A

Barn Swallow   C   (*migration*)

Gray-breasted Martin   A   (*evenings over the Hotel Bucanero and the ruins*)

Mexican Crow   A

House Wren   O*

Bar-vented Wren   O   (*near ruins*)

Happy Wren   C   (*near ruins*)

Mockingbird   C

Blue Mockingbird   C   (*very elusive*)

Rufous-backed Robin   A   (*near ruins*)

White-throated Robin   O   (*near ruins*)

Orange-billed Nightingale-Thrush   O*

Blue-Gray Gnatcatcher   A*

Black-capped Vireo   R*

Bell's Vireo   C*

Solitary Vireo   C*   (*near ruins*)

Yellow-Green Vireo   C   (*summer, near ruins*)

Warbling Vireo   C*

Black-and-White Warbler   O*

Orange-crowned Warbler   O*

Nashville Warbler   C*

Olive-backed Warbler   C   (*near ruins*)

Yellow Warbler   A

Audubon's Warbler   A*

Black-throated Gray Warbler   A*   (*near ruins*)

Ovenbird   R*

Northern Waterthrush   C*

MacGillivray's Warbler   C*

Yellowthroat   O*

Yellow-breasted Chat   C

Wilson's Warbler   A*

American Redstart   A*   (*near ruins*)

House Sparrow   C   (*in town only*)

Yellow-winged Cacique   A

Orchard Oriole   C

Hooded Oriole   A

Scarlet-headed Oriole   A

Bullock's Oriole   C*

Boat-tailed Grackle   A

Bronzed Cowbird   A
Summer Tanager   C   (*near ruins*)
Rose-breasted Thrush-Tanager   R
Grayish Saltator   A
Black-headed Grosbeak   C*
Blue Grosbeak   C   (*A during migration*)
Indigo Bunting   R*
Varied Bunting   A
Painted Bunting   C
Dickcissel   R*   (*December records*)

White-collared Seedeater   A
Ruddy-breasted Seedeater   R
Blue-Black Grassquit   R   (*A in summer*)
Lesser Goldfinch   R
Olive Sparrow   R   (*below ruins*)
Green-tailed Towhee   R*
Savannah Sparrow   R*
Stripe-headed Sparrow   O
Lincoln's Sparrow   C*
Swamp Sparrow   R*

SAN BLAS ENVIRONS TO THE WEST: THE BOOBY ROCK BOAT TRIP

A BOOBY BOAT trip over the shallow waters at the point where the estuary empties into the sea is bound to be interesting. Some boatmen will only go out at certain tides, for when the breakers are running high boats can be easily flipped. You probably should not take this trip if you can't swim or are carrying expensive optical equipment. Be prepared for salt spray.

Check for Elegant Tern on your way out to the booby rocks. The rocks are less than a mile off shore and are havens for throngs of Blue-footed Boobies and Brown Boobies and dozens of Gray-breasted Martins. If you take this trip between March and June, an unexpected sight is in store for you: dozens of pelagic Sooty Terns can be found only a mile from the mainland shore.

Instead of returning directly to the dock you may wish to go up the coast a mile to the mouth of the Estero del Rey. If your boat is able to navigate this estuary, ask your boatman to pull up to the shore so you can stroll for a few minutes on the lonely sand-spit. There is a large Least Tern colony here in the spring, and the sands are a favorite resting place for Brown Pelicans, Blue-footed Boobies, Reddish Egrets, American Oystercatchers, hundreds of plovers, sandpipers, Sanderlings, gulls, terns, and Black Skimmers.

Farther up the river you will see more waders on the mudflats, including up to a thousand Wilson's Plovers and numerous Yellow-crowned Night Herons. Your boatman will turn into a shady channel through a stand of mangroves. Another turn on the Estero del Pozo brings you back to San Blas. Look for Rufous-necked Wood Rail and Ringed Kingfisher on the return route.

Birds of San Blas II: The Booby Rock

Brown Pelican   A
Blue-footed Booby   A   (*between 30 and 120 individuals*)
Brown Booby   C   (*between 2 and 50 individuals*)
Double-crested Cormorant   O*
Magnificent Frigatebird   A
Surf Scoter   X   (*December 1965*)
Ruddy Turnstone   O*
Western Gull   O*
Bonaparte's Gull   O*

Heermann's Gull   A
Forster's Tern   C*
Common Tern   C*
Sooty Tern   A   (*March–June, up to 60 individuals*)
Least Tern   A   (*summer*)
Royal Tern   R
Elegant Tern   C
Caspian Tern   C
Gray-breasted Martin   A   (*25 to 50 pairs breed here*)

SAN BLAS ENVIRONS TO THE NORTH: THE ESTERO SAN CRISTÓBAL

ON ROUTE 54, just to the east of San Blas, a long bridge crosses the Estero San Cristóbal. In the early morning and occasionally later in the day you may see several good birds near this bridge. Look for Bare-throated Tiger Herons, Yellow-crowned Night Herons, and Boat-billed Herons beside the water. Black-bellied Tree Ducks and Muscovy Ducks might be seen in flight. Check for Lesser Scaup and Green Kingfisher. In the winter, you may find Eared Grebe in this locale.

By all means rent a boat and head up the Estero San Cristóbal. It is best to make reservations in advance, for you will want to leave at the crack of dawn. The journey to the upper reaches of the estuary where bird watching is best takes five to seven hours roundtrip. If you do not get an early start, you will miss early morning bird activity and encounter the uncomfortable afternoon sun. Facilities and conveniences are lacking on this trip, but you will welcome the complete absence of biting insects over the water.

Some of the boatmen can locate active nests of such waterbirds as Bare-throated Tiger Heron and point out Boat-billed Heron roosts in the tallest mangroves. All of them will direct your attention to the large iguanas and occasional crocodiles. Spider lilies grow in the upper reaches of the river.

As you leave the dock, the river is quite wide, making it difficult to see the birds on the shores. Remember that the diversity of land birds in the mangroves is not great and instead concentrate your attention on waterbirds, hawks, and other birds which may be seen on the wing above the wide green river.

Take the second major fork in the river to the right. Keep a special eye out for the Mangrove Cuckoo and Ringed Kingfisher. A little muddy-marshy area on the left is often thick with birds, sometimes including the Clapper Rail. A short distance farther down the river lies the first marisma, or savanna swamp. During and after the rainy season these flats fill with water and host myriads of birds in their shallows. In the spring the marismas gradually dry up, leaving remnant puddles which harbor only a few species.

As the river narrows, the water becomes fresher. You will pass several thatched homes. Notice that the mangroves grow only on the stream borders; wide marismas occupy the hinterlands on both sides.

Have your boatman pull up to the bank at every convenient approach. Get out to rest, stretch, and look for birds. When there is ample water, the numbers and varieties of birds in the marismas can be staggering. A telescope is very helpful in scanning these vast shallows.

Catch up on your land birds by following the cattle trails. Pauraques can be easily flushed, and the calls of Bar-vented Wrens, Happy Wrens, and Olive-backed Warblers are often heard in the brush.

As the sun gets higher, many birds can be seen soaring overhead in endless circles. Look for White Pelicans, Olivaceous Cormorants, Anhingas, Wood Ibis, White Ibis, Roseate Spoonbills, vultures, and such hawks as Zone-tailed, Harris', Great Black, Black, and Blackish Crane Hawks.

Birds of San Blas III: The Estero San Cristóbal and the Marismas

Eared Grebe   R*
Least Grebe   O
Pied-billed Grebe   C*
White Pelican   C*   (*in marismas*)
Double-crested Cormorant   O*
Olivaceous Cormorant   A

Anhinga   A
Magnificent Frigatebird   C
Great Blue Heron   A
Green Heron   A*
Little Blue Heron   A
Cattle Egret   C   (*in marismas*)

Common Egret   A

Snowy Egret   A

Louisiana Heron   A

Black-crowned Night Heron   A   (*near marismas*)

Yellow-crowned Night Heron   A   (*below marismas*)

Bare-throated Tiger Heron   A   (*between 2 and 13 individuals*)

Least Bittern   R

American Bittern   R*

Boat-billed Heron   A   (*roost in heavy trees beside river*)

Wood Ibis   A

White-faced Ibis   A

White Ibis   A

Roseate Spoonbill   A

Black-bellied Tree Duck   A   (*O in spring*)

Muscovy Duck   C   (*flying overhead at dawn, A in summer*)

Gadwall   A*

Pintail   A*

Green-winged Teal   A*

Blue-winged Teal   A*

Cinnamon Teal   A*

American Widgeon   A*

Shoveler   A*

Redhead   R*   (*in river*)

Lesser Scaup   C   (*in river*)

Ruddy Duck   R*

Turkey Vulture   A

Black Vulture   A

Hook-billed Kite   R

Red-tailed Hawk   C

Zone-tailed Hawk   O*

White-tailed Hawk   R

Gray Hawk   O

Harris' Hawk   C

Great Black Hawk   O

Black Hawk   A

Marsh Hawk   C*

Blackish Crane Hawk   C   (*over marismas*)

Osprey   A

Laughing Falcon   O   (*over marismas*)

Collared Forest-Falcon   R

Caracara   C

Peregrine Falcon   R*

Sparrow Hawk   R*

Sandhill Crane   X   (*October 1965*)

Clapper Rail   C

Sora Rail   C*   (*calls from reedy patches in marismas*)

Common Gallinule   A

American Coot   A*

Jacana   A   (*in marismas*)

Semipalmated Plover   C*

Collared Plover   O   (*in marismas*)

Killdeer   C

Common Snipe   O*

Long-billed Curlew   O*

Whimbrel   O*

Spotted Sandpiper   A*

Solitary Sandpiper   C*

Willet   C*

Greater Yellowlegs   A*

Lesser Yellowlegs   A*

Pectoral Sandpiper   R*   (*in marismas*)

Least Sandpiper   A*

Dowitcher, species   A*

Stilt Sandpiper   A*   (*in marismas*)

Semipalmated Sandpiper   O*

Western Sandpiper   A*

American Avocet   A*

Black-necked Stilt   A

Wilson's Phalarope   R*   (*December, 1967*)

Ring-billed Gull   R*

Forster's Tern   R*

Least Tern   O   (*summer*)

Caspian Tern   C

Red-billed Pigeon   C   (*flying overhead*)

White-winged Dove   A

Ground Dove   C

Ruddy Ground Dove   C   (*flying across river*)

White-fronted Dove   C

Ruddy Quail Dove   R   (*flying across river*)

Military Macaw   O*   (*flying overhead in the morning*)

Orange-fronted Parakeet   A

Blue-rumped Parrotlet   O

White-fronted Parrot   A

Lilac-crowned Parrot   R   (*April records*)

Mangrove Cuckoo   C

Squirrel Cuckoo   C   (*near marismas*)

Groove-billed Ani   A
Ferruginous Owl   O
Pauraque   C
Vaux's Swift   R*
Cinnamon Hummingbird   A
Citreoline Trogon   O
Coppery-tailed Trogon   R
Belted Kingfisher   A*
Ringed Kingfisher   C
Amazon Kingfisher   R
Green Kingfisher   A   (*Between 10 and 45 individuals*)
Linneated Woodpecker   C
Golden-cheeked Woodpecker   A
Ladder-backed Woodpecker   O
Pale-billed Woodpecker   C
Ivory-billed Woodcreeper   O
Rose-throated Becard   R
Masked Tityra   C
Tropical Kingbird   A
Thick-billed Kingbird   A
Social Flycatcher   A
Kiskadee Flycatcher   A
Olivaceous Flycatcher   C
Wied's Crested Flycatcher   R
Empidonax, species   O
Coues' Flycatcher   R*
Vermilion Flycatcher   C
Mangrove Swallow   A
Rough-winged Swallow   A
Barn Swallow   C   (*migration*)
San Blas Jay   O
Magpie-Jay   O
Mexican Crow   C

Mockingbird   O
Blue Mockingbird   R
Bar-vented Wren   C
Happy Wren   O
Rufous-backed Robin   O
Blue-Gray Gnatcatcher   C*
White-lored Gnatcatcher   R
Water Pipit   O*
Mangrove Vireo   O
Black-and-White Warbler   O*
Orange-crowned Warbler   O*
Olive-backed Warbler   O
Yellow Warbler   A
Audubon's Warbler   O*
Northern Waterthrush   A*
MacGillivray's Warbler   C*
Yellowthroat   C*
Yellow-breasted Chat   C
Wilson's Warbler   A*
American Redstart   A*
Yellow-winged Cacique   A
Red-winged Blackbird   C
Orchard Oriole   O
Scarlet-headed Oriole   A
Baltimore Oriole   R*
Boat-tailed Grackle   A
Bronzed Cowbird   C
Summer Tanager   R
Grayish Saltator   C
Black-headed Grosbeak   R*
Painted Bunting   C
White-collared Seedeater   C
Blue-Black Grassquit   A   (*R in winter*)
Lincoln's Sparrow   C*

SAN BLAS ENVIRONS TO THE EAST: THE SEASONAL LAGOONS

To explore the environs to the east, take Route 54 out of town, retracing the road you took coming in, all the way to the hill above Singaita. Your first stop should be the mangrove forests just beyond the Rio San Cristóbal bridge. Keep an eye out for Ivory-billed Woodcreeper and in the winter, Northern Waterthrush and American Redstart.

Beyond the mangroves lie many treeless expanses. These are bone-dry in the spring until the coming of the rains. When the rainwaters transform these flats into shallow lagoons, thick populations of birds infest the area. On early mornings in the fall, winter, and sometimes in the spring, from a distance the waters may appear to be white, pink, or another striking shade, due to the masses of wading birds feeding here. In the summer a huge rookery beyond one of the lagoons on the south side of the road abounds with Olivaceous Cormorants, Anhingas, Little Blue Herons, Common Egrets, Snowy Egrets, and Louisiana Herons.

Birds of San Blas IV: The Seasonal Lagoons

Note: This bird list is not accurate for the spring dry season.

Least Grebe   R
Pied-billed Grebe   R*
Olivaceous Cormorant   A
Anhinga   A
Great Blue Heron   C
Green Heron   A*
Little Blue Heron   A
Cattle Egret   R
Common Egret   A
Snowy Egret   A
Louisiana Heron   A
Yellow-crowned Night Heron   A
Bare-throated Tiger Heron   R
Boat-billed Heron   R
Wood Ibis   C
White-faced Ibis   O
White Ibis   A
Roseate Spoonbill   C
Black-bellied Tree Duck   C
Muscovy Duck   C   (*overhead at dawn*)
Gadwall   C*
Pintail   C*
Green-winged Teal   A*
Blue-winged Teal   C*
Cinnamon Teal   C*
American Widgeon   C*
Shoveler   C*
Ruddy Duck   R*
Turkey Vulture   A
Black Vulture   A
Zone-tailed Hawk   O*
Short-tailed Hawk   R
Harris' Hawk   R
Black Hawk   C
Great Black Hawk   R
Osprey   O
Caracara   O
Sparrow Hawk   C*
Clapper Rail   O
Sora   O
Common Gallinule   C
American Coot   A*
Jacana   O
Semipalmated Plover   A*
Collared Plover   R

Wilson's Plover   C
Killdeer   C
Common Snipe   O*
Long-billed Curlew   C*
Whimbrel   C*
Spotted Sandpiper   A*
Solitary Sandpiper   O*
Willet   A*
Greater Yellowlegs   A*
Lesser Yellowlegs   A*
Least Sandpiper   A*
Short-billed Dowitcher   A*
Long-billed Dowitcher   A*
Stilt Sandpiper   C*
Semipalmated Sandpiper   C*
Western Sandpiper   A*
Marbled Godwit   C*
American Avocet   A*
Black-necked Stilt   A
Caspian Tern   O
Black Skimmer   R
Red-billed Pigeon   O
White-winged Dove   A
Ground Dove   A
Ruddy Ground Dove   C
Orange-fronted Parakeet   O
White-fronted Parrot   A
Mangrove Cuckoo   R
Groove-billed Ani   C
Pauraque   O   (*night*)
Lesser Nighthawk   R
Cinnamon Hummingbird   O
Belted Kingfisher   A*
Ringed Kingfisher   O
Green Kingfisher   C
Golden-cheeked Woodpecker   C
Ivory-billed Woodcreeper   O
Tropical Kingbird   A
Social Flycatcher   A
Kiskadee Flycatcher   A
Vermilion Flycatcher   C*
Mangrove Swallow   A
Rough-winged Swallow   C
Bar-vented Wren   O
Mockingbird   C

Rufous-backed Robin   O
Blue-Gray Gnatcatcher   C*
Water Pipit   C*
Mangrove Vireo   O
Orange-crowned Warbler   C*
Nashville Warbler   C*
Yellow Warbler   C
Northern Waterthrush   C*
Yellowthroat   C*
Wilson's Warbler   C*

American Redstart   A*
Yellow-winged   Cacique   A   (*in   huge   flocks   at   dawn*)
Orchard Oriole   C*
Scarlet-headed Oriole   C
Boat-tailed Grackle   A
Blue Grosbeak   O*
Painted Bunting   C
Lincoln's Sparrow   C*

SAN BLAS ENVIRONS TO THE EAST: THE SAN BLAS-SINGAITA JUNGLE

Beyond the flats of the seasonal lagoons, lush jungles cover the inland hills. Authorities debate on whether to call this growth tropical deciduous forest or tropical evergreen forest. In actuality, it must be considered transitional, for representative species of both classifications grow here side by side.

A particularly heavy concentration of oil-nut palms and various tall figs, eardrop trees, gumbolimbos, and kapoks give the jungle a height and thickness that dwarfs the deciduous forests to the north. There is an abundance of undergrowth as in a true jungle, unlike the typical rain forest.

The jungle is only a ten-minute drive from San Blas, beyond the little village of Singaita. At present it is one of the few accessible natural forest habitats in Mexico's tropics. It can only be hoped that increasing needs for marginal farmlands do not cause man to transform this rich natural vegetation into acres of cornfields.

Your first impulse will be to find a trail and head into the forest, but experience has shown this approach to be unrewarding. By doing your bird watching along the road you gain several advantages. Birds seem to be less shy along the road than they do inside the jungle. Roadside vegetation is more diverse than vegetation inside the forest because sunlight is more abundant in the open area. Much better visibility on all sides can be had from the road, and the telephone wires are good, easy-to-spot perches. If you always walk downhill and keep your group to one side of the road whenever a vehicle passes, you will have an optimal and safe experience in jungle bird watching.

Always start at the crack of dawn when bird activity and song are at their height. Retire before 10:30 when the forest becomes hot and quiet, perhaps returning for another stroll in the cool of the evening. It is recommended that you be sure to cover each section of the road several different times, for some birds seem to be localized in specific areas, and it is not possible to see all species in one bird watching session.

Your bird watching will be enriched by many exotic sights and sounds. Gray squirrels are common and make much noise as they jump between the palm fronds. Colorful butterflies of many species flutter through the air, and long lines of leaf-cutter ants carry large leaves across the road. Jungle mammals and reptiles seldom venture out of the inner forest, although a dazed boa constrictor was found beside the road on a recent bird watching trip.

Begin your jungle bird watching on the summit of the hill which rises just to the east of Singaita, then gradually descend the slope and progress towards San Blas. The hillside forest is thick on both sides of the road and can be designated "upper jungle" as distinguished from the more open "lower jungle" west of Singaita.

The most elevated inland edge of the thick upper jungle is one of the richest and most active spots for birds. It is the only section where you can find Crested Guan, Gray-crowned Woodpecker, Green Jay, and Black-vented Oriole. The first ravine you pass going downhill is the best place to look for the Fan-tailed Warbler. Other species inhabiting this area are Military Macaw, Orange-fronted Parakeet, Blue-rumped Parrotlet, White-fronted Parrot, Lilac-crowned Parrot, Squirrel Cuckoo, Long-tailed Hermit, Russet-crowned Motmot, Tufted Flycatcher (winter), Blue Mockingbird, White-throated Robin, Orange-billed Nightingale-Thrush, Golden Vireo, and Red-crowned Ant-Tanager.

Many birds from the eastern United States which normally winter in or migrate through eastern Mexico, Central America, and South America have been found in this jungle. Most bird lists assign them accidental status, although it is suspected that they are actually more common than collectors have indicated to this date.

If you feel that you cannot resist penetrating the strangeness of the inner jungle, there is an accessible area. Take the dirt and rock road which branches south off of Route 54 a few turns up the hill above Singaita. It leads to an open area where you can stroll with little difficulty and probably see Ground Chats, but be prepared for inevitable chiggers and other irritations.

A lively stream comes out of the jungle at Singaita, forming a little pond that attracts Ground Chats and Jacanas. From here on you will be in the lower jungle, which stretches to the mangrove swamps on the south side of the road. Fields, scrub, and mangrove trees occupy the north side. Blue-rumped Parrotlets, Bright-rumped Attilas, Greenish Elaenias, Orchard Orioles, and a variety of finches are more likely to be seen here than in the thicker upper jungle. As you come out of Singaita, just before you reach the first mangrove trees on your right, look for a sleeping Ferruginous Owl which makes its home in this stretch of the jungle.

Birds of San Blas V: The San Blas-Singaita Jungle

Rufescent Tinamou   O   (*gives a quivering double note*)
Wood Ibis   R   (*Singaita pond*)
White-faced Ibis   R   (*Singaita pond*)
Black-bellied Tree Duck   O   (*nests in forest trees in early summer*)
Turkey Vulture   A
Black Vulture   A
Sharp-shinned Hawk   R*
Cooper's Hawk   C*
Red-tailed Hawk   R
Zone-tailed Hawk   O*
Short-tailed Hawk   C   (*a recent discovery, both dark and light phases*)
Gray Hawk   C
Black Hawk   A
Great Black Hawk   O
Blackish Crane Hawk   R
Laughing Falcon   R
Collared Forest-Falcon   R

Caracara   O
Bat Falcon   R
Sparrow Hawk   R*
Crested Guan   R   (*April record*)
Rufous-bellied Chachalaca   C   (*very noisy at dawn some days*)
Jacana   O   (*Singaita pond*)
Red-billed Pigeon   C
White-winged Dove   A   (*huge flocks fly inland most mornings*)
Ground Dove   A
Ruddy Ground Dove   C
White-fronted Dove   A   (*flushes often from the roadside*)
Ruddy Quail Dove   R   (*flies across road*)
Military Macaw   O*   (*small groups fly inland in the morning*)
Orange-fronted Parakeet   A
Blue-rumped Parrotlet   A
White-fronted Parrot   A

HIGHLAND SONGBIRDS

male

female

Blue-hooded Euphonia
Tanagra musica

male

female

Pale-vented Euphonia
Tanagra affinis godmani

male

female

Red-breasted Chat
Granatellus venustus

Brown-backed Solitaire
Myadestes obscurus

Slate-throated Redstart
Myioborus miniatus

Russet Nightingale-Thrush
Catharus occidentalis

Orange-billed Nightingale-Thrush
Catharus aurantiirostris

Golden-browed Warbler
Basileuterus belli

Red Warbler
Ergaticus ruber

Rufous-capped Warbler
Basileuterus rufifrons

Gray Silky Flycatcher
Ptilogonys cinereus

scent-chested Warbler
ivora superciliosa

Red-headed Tanager
Piranga erythrocephala

Flame-colored Tanager
Piranga bidentata

Lilac-crowned Parrot   A
Squirrel Cuckoo   C
Groove-billed Ani   A
Ferruginous Owl   O
Common Potoo   R
Pauraque   R
Vaux's Swift   A*   (*flocks fly overhead*)
Long-tailed Hermit   C*
Plain-capped Star-throat   C
Berylline Hummingbird   R
Cinnamon Hummingbird   A
Fork-tailed Emerald   O
Broad-billed Hummingbird   A
Citreoline Trogon   A
Coppery-tailed Trogon   A
Russet-crowned Motmot   A   (*Trace its loud double hoots. If you imitate them well, you may draw the bird to you.*)
Gray-crowned Woodpecker   O
Linneated Woodpecker   A
Golden-cheeked Woodpecker   A
Smoky-Brown Woodpecker   R (Brown)
Ladder-backed Woodpecker   O
Pale-billed Woodpecker   A
Ivory-billed Woodcreeper   A
Bright-rumped Attila   R
Gray-collared Becard   R
Rose-throated Becard   A
Masked Tityra   A
Tropical Kingbird   A
Thick-billed Kingbird   C
Boat-billed Flycatcher   C
Social Flycatcher   A
Kiskadee Flycatcher   A
Sulphur-bellied Flycatcher   A   (*summer*)
Wied's Crested Flycatcher   O
Ash-throated/Nutting's Flycatcher   C
Olivaceous Flycatcher   A
Flammulated Flycatcher   R
Western Flycatcher   A*
Empidonax, species   A*
Tufted Flycatcher   O*
Coues' Flycatcher   A*
Western Wood Pewee   C*
Vermilion Flycatcher   O   (*Singaita*)
Greenish Elaenia   R
Beardless Flycatcher   A
Green Jay   R
San Blas Jay   R

Magpie-Jay   C
Mexican Crow   A   (*Signaita*)
Bar-vented Wren   A   (*stays near ground, elusive*)
Happy Wren   A   (*stays near ground, elusive*)
Mockingbird   R
Blue Mockingbird   A   (*elusive*)
Rufous-backed Robin   A
White-throated Robin   C
Hermit Thrush   C*
Swainson's Thrush   C*   (*A in April*)
Orange-billed Nightingale Thrush   O   (*December and April records*)
Blue-Gray Gnatcatcher   A*
Ruby-crowned Kinglet   R*
Black-capped Vireo   C*
Mangrove Vireo   R
Golden Vireo   O   (*between 5 and 20 feet high in trees*)
Yellow-throated Vireo   X   (*December 1961*)
Solitary Vireo   A*
Yellow-Green Vireo   A   (*summer*)
Philadelphia Vireo   R*
Warbling Vireo   A*
Black-and-White Warbler   C*
Worm-eating Warbler   X   (*October 1965*)
Tennessee Warbler   R*
Orange-crowned Warbler   A*
Nashville Warbler   A*
Lucy's Warbler   R   (*migration*)
Olive-backed Warbler   A   (*stays high in trees*)
Yellow Warbler   A*
Audubon's Warbler   C*
Black-throated Gray Warbler   A*
Palm Warbler   X   (*December 1964*)
Ovenbird   R*
Northern Waterthrush   O*
Louisiana Waterthrush   R*
Kentucky Warbler   X   (*March 1964*)
MacGillivray's Warbler   A*
Ground Chat   O   (*Singaita pond*)
Yellow-breasted Chat   A
Red-breasted Chat   R   (*December record*)
Fan-tailed Warbler   O
Hooded Warbler   X   (*March 1964*)

Wilson's Warbler   A*
American Redstart   A*
Yellow-winged Cacique   A
Orchard Oriole   O   (*Singaita area*)
Hooded Oriole   O
Scarlet-headed Oriole   A
Black-vented Oriole   O
Bullock's Oriole   C*
Boat-tailed Grackle   A
Bronzed Cowbird   A   (*Singaita area*)
Pale-vented Euphonia   C   (*high in broad-leafed trees*)
Western Tanager   O   (*late April*)
Scarlet Tanager   X   (*December 1961*)
Summer Tanager   A
Red-crowned   Ant-Tanager   A   (*usually near the ground, elusive*)

Rose-throated Thrush-Tanager   R
Grayish Saltator   A
Yellow Grosbeak   C
Rose-breasted   Grosbeak   X   (*December 1965*)
Black-headed Grosbeak   C*
Blue Grosbeak   C
Blue Bunting   C
Indigo Bunting   O*
Varied Bunting   C
Painted Bunting   C
Dickcissel   R*
White-collared Seedeater   C
Blue-Black Grassquit   C
Lesser Goldfinch   R*
Rusty-crowned Ground Sparrow   C   (*usually on the ground, elusive*)

SAN BLAS ENVIRONS TO THE SOUTH: THE MATANCHEN BAY AREA

A highlight of your western Mexico bird watching expedition will be the popular jungle river boat trip. Boats which embark from the Estero San Cristóbal bridge take a long route and are fairly expensive to rent. The great majority of boats leave from La Aguada, a small group of huts about a mile and a half to the south near Matanchen Bay. The trip from La Aguada is shorter, less expensive, and just as good for birds.

Take Route 54 east out of town and turn south on the good dirt road to La Aguada. Birds are quite sparse along this route, although Bar-vented Wrens, Northern Waterthrushes, and American Redstarts are common in season, and Mangrove Cuckoos and Citreoline Trogons can sometimes be seen crossing the road. At night your headlights will probably flash upon the beady red eyes of resting Pauraques.

The jungle boat ride is quite popular with tourists, and during the day the heavy river traffic scares most birds into the jungle. Take the trip at dawn or in the evening to catch the full activity of the bird life here.

After leaving the docks at La Aguada, your boat will wind through several miles of cool, shady mangroves. These gradually give way to tall, grassy marshland. Your destination is La Tovara a deep, clear freshwater spring bubbling up from a thickly forested hill. Here you will relax and perhaps take a swim before making the return trip.

If you take the trip at dawn, keep your eyes open for Anhingas, Bare-throated Tiger Herons, Boat-billed Herons, Black-bellied Tree Ducks, wintering Zone-tailed Hawks, Rufous-necked Wood Rails (rarely seen, in mangroves), Purple Gallinules (rare), Common Gallinules, Jacanas, Citreoline Trogons, kingfishers (Belted, Green, and sometimes Ringed and Amazon), Rufous-backed Robins, Yellow (Mangrove) Warblers, and American Redstarts.

An evening trip will be mysteriously beautiful and require different bird watching techniques. It is most important to bring along a strong flashlight.

Arrange to take the trip at sunset. On your way upstream, look for Muscovy Ducks and Rufous-bellied Chachalacas in addition to the species mentioned above. Relax at La Tovara until it is completely dark and the last tourists have gone back to

La Aguada. Ask your boatman to return downstream slowly and quietly, without the motor if possible. Look for crocodiles and big catfish in the clear waters. Large sleeping iguanas can be seen on top of the low streamside trees. It is an obvious precaution to resist the temptation of trailing your fingers in the cool waters.

Scan your flashlight across the tops of the tall trees to see the bright reddish-orange eyes of Common Potoos perched on dead limbs, waiting for moths to fly by. These birds are much larger than any Goatsucker. If you find one perched beside the water, you can almost touch the mysterious bird before it flies off. Up to fifteen Common Potoos may be seen on a night trip downstream.

Pauraques on the wing or perched on sticks beside the water can be spotted by using your flashlight to catch the red reflection of their eyes. Mottled Owls occur in the trees, but must be distinguished by their form, as their eyes do not seem to reflect any color from a flashlight beam.

Your boat will awaken many other birds beside the stream. Numerous Tropical Kingbirds and Social Flycatchers will stir in the tall heavy grasses. A silent, motionless Least Bittern might be glimpsed in the vegetation. Nearer the water you will probably see Common Gallinules, Jacanas, and Northern Waterthrushes.

Look for Green Kingfishers sleeping on little branches about a foot above the water. You can easily reach up and take them in your hand, although this usually wakes them. Be sure to keep your fingers away from their bills.

* * *

Back in La Aguada, be sure to do some more bird watching around the bay area. The Hotel Colon is situated on the beach and often has a flock of Gray-breasted Martins over it. You can drive from the hotel out on the hard-packed sand and follow the beach towards the sea. Look for Ruddy Ground Doves, Mangrove Swallows, and wintering Savannah Sparrows in the beach grass. Snowy Plovers, Wilson's Plovers, and wintering Black-bellied Plovers can be seen on the sand. At low tide the sandbar will be covered with herons, plovers, shorebirds, gulls, and terns. Look especially for Reddish Egrets, American Oystercatchers, Ruddy Turnstones, Long-billed Curlews, Whimbrels, Marbled Godwits, American Avocets, Black Skimmers, and Gull-billed, Forster's, Common, Least, Royal, Elegant, and Caspian Terns.

The beach road crosses back through the grass to three lovely half-moon beaches, one of Mexico's least publicized beauty spots. Over the waters you will see Brown Pelicans, Blue-footed Boobies, Olivaceous Cormorants, Magnificent Frigatebirds, Ospreys, and various gulls and terns. Occasionally in the winter you can spot Surf Scoters and Peregrine Falcons in the bay. On the rocky points, wintering Surfbirds, Ruddy Turnstones and more rarely, Black Turnstones, may be seen.

Just beyond the parking shed opposite the Hotel Colon is a dirt road going right (west). If you have the time, stroll along it, looking for various land birds. Take the first righthand fork northwest to a banana plantation. Dozens of Ruddy Ground Doves and Painted Buntings sometimes can be seen in the weeds. The pond is a good place to look for Least Grebes, Pied-billed Grebes, Jacanas, Solitary Sandpipers, and Black-necked Stilts. A large crocodile often snoozes on an island in the water. In the trees around the pond you may see several Citreoline Trogons.

The road takes you past more banana trees into a tall mangrove forest. Check for Red-billed Pigeons, White-fronted Doves, Orange-fronted Parakeets, Squirrel Cuckoos, Cinnamon Hummingbirds, Ivory-billed Woodcreepers, Beardless Flycatchers, Rufous-backed Robins, wintering Black-and-White Warblers, the Yellow-breasted Chats, Yellow-winged Caciques, and Grayish Saltators. White-collared Seedeaters may be spotted in the weedy areas.

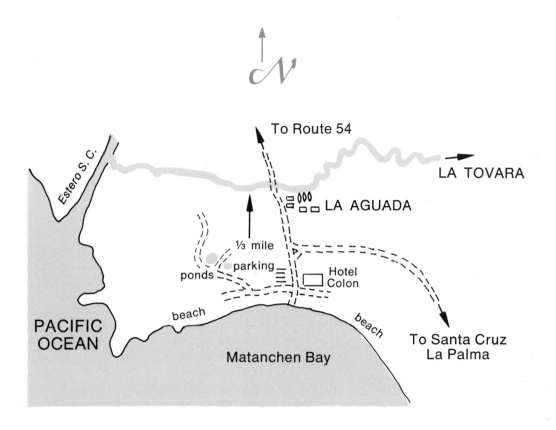

**SAN BLAS— South
La Aquada Area**

Birds of San Blas VI: Boat Trip to La Tovara and the Matanchen Bay Area

Least Grebe   O   (*in pond*)
Pied-billed Grebe   R*   (*in pond*)
Brown Pelican   A
Blue-footed Booby   A
Brown Booby   C
Olivaceous Cormorant   A
Anhinga   O
Magnificent Frigatebird   A
Great Blue Heron   C
Green Heron   A
Little Blue Heron   O
Reddish Egret   C
Common Egret   C
Snowy Egret   A
Louisiana Heron   C
Yellow-crowned Night Heron   O
Bare-throated Tiger Heron   R
Least Bittern   O
Boat-billed Heron   O
Wood Ibis   O
White-faced Ibis   R
White Ibis   A
Roseate Spoonbill   O
Black-bellied Tree Duck   O
Muscovy Duck   R
Gadwall   R*
Pintail   O*
Blue-winged Teal   O*   (*in pond*)
Shoveler   O*
Lesser Scaup   R*
Surf Scoter   X   (*December 1965*)
Turkey Vulture   A
Black Vulture   A
Zone-tailed Hawk   O*
Short-tailed Hawk   R
Black Hawk   C
Osprey   A
Caracara   R
Peregrine Falcon   R*
Rufous-bellied Chachalaca   R
Rufous-necked Wood-Rail   R
Purple Gallinule   R
Common Gallinule   A
American Coot   C*
Jacana   C
American Oystercatcher   O

Semipalmated Plover   C*
Snowy Plover   O
Collared Plover   R
Wilson's Plover   A
Killdeer   R*
Black-bellied Plover   A*
Surfbird   O*
Ruddy Turnstone   A*
Black Turnstone   R*
Common Snipe   R*
Long-billed Curlew   C*
Whimbrel   C*
Spotted Sandpiper   A*
Solitary Sandpiper   O*
Wandering Tattler   R*
Willet   A
Greater Yellowlegs   O*
Lesser Yellowlegs   R*
Least Sandpiper   C*
Western Sandpiper   O*
Marbled Godwit   A*
Sanderling   A*
American Avocet   C*
Black-necked Stilt   C
Ring-billed Gull   A*
Laughing Gull   C
Heermann's Gull   A
Gull-billed Tern   O
Forster's Tern   A*
Common Tern   A*
Least Tern   A   (*summer*)
Royal Tern   R
Elegant Tern   O
Caspian Tern   O
Black Skimmer   O
Red-billed Pigeon   C
White-winged Dove   A
Ground Dove   A
Ruddy Ground Dove   A
Mourning Dove   R*
White-fronted Dove   O
Orange-fronted Parakeet   A
Blue-rumped Parrotlet   O
White-fronted Parrot   A
Lilac-crowned Parrot   R
Mangrove Cuckoo   R

Squirrel Cuckoo   O
Groove-billed Ani   A
Ferruginous Owl   R
Mottled Owl   R   (*night*)
Common Potoo   A   (*night*)
Pauraque   C   (*night*)
Vaux's Swift   O*
Cinnamon Hummingbird   C
Broad-billed Hummingbird   O*
Citreoline Trogon   C
Belted Kingfisher   A*
Ringed Kingfisher   R
Amazon Kingfisher   R
Green Kingfisher   C
Russet-crowned Motmot   R
Linneated Woodpecker   R
Golden-cheeked Woodpecker   A
Ivory-billed Woodcreeper   C
Rose-throated Becard   O
Masked Tityra   O
Tropical Kingbird   A
Thick-billed Kingbird   O
Social Flycatcher   A
Kiskadee Flycatcher   A
Vermilion Flycatcher   R*
Beardless Flycatcher
Mangrove Swallow   A
Rough-winged Swallow   Λ
Gray-breasted Martin   C
Mexican Crow   C
House Wren   O*
Bar-vented Wren   C
Happy Wren   R
Mockingbird   O

Blue Mockingbird   R
Rufous-backed Robin   O
Blue-Gray Gnatcatcher   C*
Black-capped Vireo   R*
Mangrove Vireo   R
Solitary Vireo   O*
Warbling Vireo   C*
Black-and-White Warbler   O*
Orange-crowned Warbler   A*
Nashville Warbler   C*
Olive-backed Warbler   C
Yellow Warbler   C
Northern Waterthrush   C*
Louisiana Waterthrush   R*
MacGillivray's Warbler   C*
Yellow-breasted Chat   C
Wilson's Warbler   A*
American Redstart   A*
Yellow-winged Cacique   C
Orchard Oriole   O*
Scarlet-headed Oriole   A
Boat-tailed Grackle   A
Bronzed Cowbird   A
Pale-vented Euphonia   R   (Scrub)
Summer Tanager   O*
Grayish Saltator   C
Blue Grosbeak   O
Varied Bunting   O
Painted Bunting   O
White-collared Seedeater   A
Blue-Black Grassquit   O
Savannah Sparrow   C*
Lincoln's Sparrow   C*

THE CAMINO REAL: LA PALMA TO JALCOCOTÁN

PAST LA AGUADA near Matanchen Bay, just before you reach the Hotel Colon, a sign indicates a dirt road which travels down the coast to Playa Los Cocos and Santa Cruz. If possible, save a morning to drive south on this route which cuts between the long shoreline of Matanchen Bay and lush coconut plantations. Check the beach for the usual waterbirds, particularly the Snowy Plover. Look in the weeds for Ground Dove, Ruddy Ground Dove, Blue Grosbeak, White-collared Seedeater, and various buntings.

After driving several miles you will arrive at a jungle-covered bluff overlooking the sea. The road turns inland at this point. Some small ponds on the left may have Bare-throated Tiger Herons, White-faced Ibis, various ducks, and other waterbirds.

After driving inland through about a mile of palm forest, you will reach a junction. If you go straight you will pass through Santa

Cruz where you can catch Route 66 East to Tepic. The left (inland) branch, a part of the old Camino Real between San Blas and Jalcocotán, takes you through the villages of La Palma and La Bajada, climbs through some steep hills covered with coffee and banana plantations, and finally joins Route 66 about a mile from Jalcocotán.

Do not attempt the Camino Real unless you have a special vehicle. The ancient cobblestone and dirt surface is kept in good order, but the road is often very steep, and the jungle can be quite heavy. It is safest to drive to Tepic or Jalcocotán, then take the Camino Real downhill.

Coming downhill from Jalcocotán, turn right (northwest) at the little green shrine. The road passes through coffee and banana plantations, sometimes flanked by volcanic cinder cones. One of the best bird watching areas in western Mexico lies in the coffee plantations about three miles away from the highway. Coffee in Mexico must be grown in shade, a fact which puts the coffee tree in first place as a desirable crop from a conservationist's view. These tall jungle giants, along with the tropical fig and the gumbo-limbo, suggest what much of coastal Nayarit must have been before the coming of the axe and agriculture. Banana plantations, on the other hand, have a paucity of birds, even though some practical owners are planting coffee in the shade of the banana trees.

The Camino Real winds through various other habitats before it descends into a cool, solid canopy of trees shading more coffee plantations. Here you can walk on ancient cobblestones through the dark forest, catching dramatic glimpses of the bright blue Pacific through the trees.

The first village you will encounter is La Bajada. After passing through more forest and crossing a few rushing streams, you will arrive at La Palma. The inland edge of this village has a Stripe-headed Sparrow colony on the north side of the road. The Matanchen-Santa Cruz road joins the Camino Real several hundred yards beyond La Palma.

Birds of San Blas VII: The Camino Real: La Palma to Jalcocotán

Black Vulture   A
Turkey Vulture   A
Red-tailed Hawk   R
Zone-tailed Hawk   R*
Short-tailed Hawk   O
Gray Hawk   C
Rufous-bellied Chachalaca   R
Elegant Quail   R
Red-billed Pigeon   O
White-winged Dove   A
Ground Dove   C
Ruddy Ground Dove   C
Inca Dove   O
White-fronted Dove   C
Ruddy Quail Dove   O   (*coffee plantations*)
Orange-fronted Parakeet   A
Blue-rumped Parrotlet   O
White-fronted Parrot   A
Lilac-crowned Parrot   C
Squirrel Cuckoo   O

Groove-billed Ani   A
Mottled Owl   R
Plain-capped Star-throat   O
Violet-crowned Hummingbird   O
Berylline Hummingbird   C
Cinnamon Hummingbird   A
Fork-tailed Emerald   O
Broad-billed Hummingbird   C
Coppery-tailed Trogon   C
Citreoline Trogon   O
Russet-crowned Motmot   O
Gray-crowned Woodpecker   O
Linneated Woodpecker   C
Golden-cheeked Woodpecker   A
Pale-billed Woodpecker   C
Ivory-billed Woodcreeper   C
Rose-throated Becard   O
Masked Tityra   A
Tropical Kingbird   A
Boat-billed Flycatcher   C
Social Flycatcher   O

WARBLERS, ORIOLES, TANAGERS, VIREO, CACIQUE

Yellow-winged Cacique
Cassiculus melanicterus

female

male

Red-crowned Ant-Tanager
Habia rubica

Scarlet-headed Oriole
Icterus pustulatus

Black-vented Oriole
Icterus wagleri

Golden Vireo
Vireo hypochryseus

female

male

Rose-breasted Thrush-Tanager
Rhodinocichla rosea

**Yellow Warbler
(red-headed race)**
*Dendroica petechia
rhizophorae*

Fan-tailed Warbler
Euthlypis lachrymosa

Sulphur-bellied Flycatcher   A   (*summer*)
Olivaceous Flycatcher   C
Tufted Flycatcher   R*
Coues' Flycatcher   C*
Green Jay   R
San Blas Jay   C   (*elusive*)
Bar-vented Wren   R
Happy Wren   C
Blue Mockingbird   R
Rufous-backed Robin   C
White-throated Robin   C
Orange-billed Nightingale Thrush   O*
Blue-Gray Gnatcatcher   A*
Black-capped Vireo   O*
Golden Vireo   O
Solitary Vireo   C*
Yellow-Green Vireo   A   (*summer*)
Warbling Vireo   C*
Black-and-White Warbler   O*
Orange-crowned Warbler   C*
Olive-backed Warbler   C
Nashville Warbler   A*
Virginia's Warbler   R*
Black-throated Gray Warbler   C*
Black-throated Green Warbler   X   (*December, 1967*)
Chestnut-sided Warbler   X   (*December, 1967*)
MacGillivray's Warbler   A*
Wilson's Warbler   A*

Louisiana Waterthrush   O*
American Redstart   O*
Yellow-winged Cacique   A
Orchard Oriole   C
Hooded Oriole   C
Scarlet-headed Oriole   A
Black-vented Oriole   O
Baltimore Oriole   R*
Bullock's Oriole   C*
Boat-tailed Grackle   A
Pale-vented Euphonia   R (*scrub*)
Western Tanager   A   (*late April*)
Summer Tanager   A
Red-crowned Ant-Tanager   A
Grayish Saltator   A
Yellow Grosbeak   C
Black-headed Grosbeak   C*
Blue Grosbeak   A
Indigo Bunting   C*
Varied Bunting   A
Painted Bunting   C
White-collared Seedeater   A
Ruddy-breasted Seedeater   R
Blue-Black Grassquit   C
Lesser Goldfinch   A
Olive Sparrow   R
Rusty-crowned Ground Sparrow   C
Stripe-headed Sparrow   A   (*in brush on inland edge of La Palma*)

ROUTE 15: CRUCERO SAN BLAS TO TEPIC

IF YOU HAVE TAKEN the suggested side trip down the coast towards Santa Cruz, you will probably want to take Route 66 east to Tepic and catch this part of Route 15 on your way back north. If you are still in San Blas, return to Route 15 via Route 54 East. The spectacular sights along this stretch of Route 15 make it a recommended part of your trip.

The highway climbs steeply up to the heights of Tepic, the capitol of Nayarit, 3000 feet above sea level. About three miles outside of Crucero San Blas you will come to a sign which says "JUMATÁN-LA PLANTA HYDROELECTRICO." Take the paved road which branches west here. You will pass through some fine deciduous forest with several streams flowing through it. Park in the village of Jumatán, then walk to the pond and look at the impressive, misty waterfall which plunges over the ridge during all months but those in the dry season. Bird watching is good in this area; if you have time stroll down the forest road, looking for the species in the facing list.

Four miles farther south on Route 15 is the magnificent barranca Mirador El Aguila. The highway passes the barranca on a dangerous blind curve. It is wisest to continue past it, then turn around and approach it from the south. There is ample parking near the canyon.

The steep, rough canyon walls will prevent much walking, and biting insects can be quite irritating. It is best to simply sit on the concrete wall and view the spectacle below you.

Military Macaws fly back and forth between the canyon walls, screaming loudly.

This is the only place in west Mexico where the Great Swallow-tailed Swift has been seen. Keep an eye out for it winging across the barranca.

The remainder of Route 15 to Tepic travels through rather open country. As you approach the city you will welcome the cool, refreshing air of the pine mountains.

Birds Between Crucero San Blas and Tepic: The Barranca Country, Mirador El Aguila, and the Planta Hydroelectrico at Jumatán

Rufescent Tinamou   R
Swainson's Hawk   A   (*migration*)
Zone-tailed Hawk   O
Short-tailed Hawk   C
White-tailed Hawk   R
Gray Hawk   C
Black Hawk   R
Rufous-bellied Chachalaca   O
Elegant Quail   O
Jacana   C   (*Jumatán pond*)
Military Macaw   C   (*R in summer*)
Orange-fronted Parakeet   A
Blue-rumped Parrotlet   C
White-fronted Parrot   A
Lilac-crowned Parrot   A
Squirrel Cuckoo   O
Lesser Ground Cuckoo   R
Lesser Roadrunner   O
Groove-billed Ani   C
White-naped Swift   O*
Black Swift   C*
Great Swallow-tailed Swift   X   (*April 15, 1967—two over Mirador El Aguila*)
Berylline Hummingbird   O
Cinnamon Hummingbird   A
Fork-tailed Emerald   C
Broad-billed Hummingbird   A
Citreoline Trogon   O
Russet-crowned Motmot   O
Golden-cheeked Woodpecker   A
Pale-billed Woodpecker   O
Masked Tityra   C

Tropical Kingbird   A
Thick-billed Kingbird   A
Boat-billed Flycatcher   O
Social Flycatcher   C
Kiskadee Flycatcher   C
Magpie-Jay   A
Common Raven   C
Mexican Crow   C
Happy Wren   C
Canyon Wren   O
Rufous-backed Robin   O
Brown-backed Solitaire   C   (*calls from the Mirador El Aguila*)
Black-capped Vireo   C*
Yellow-Green Vireo   A   (*summer*)
Black-and-White Warbler   R*
Olive-backed Warbler   R
Yellow-breasted Chat   O
Yellow-winged Cacique   A
Scarlet-headed Oriole   A
Black-vented Oriole   C
Grayish Saltator   O
Yellow Grosbeak   O
Black-headed Grosbeak   O*
Blue Grosbeak   C*
Blue Bunting   R
Varied Bunting   C
Painted Bunting   C
White-collared Seedeater   C
Blue-Black Grassquit   C
Rusty-crowned Ground Sparrow   C
Botteri's Sparrow   R   (*grassy fields*)

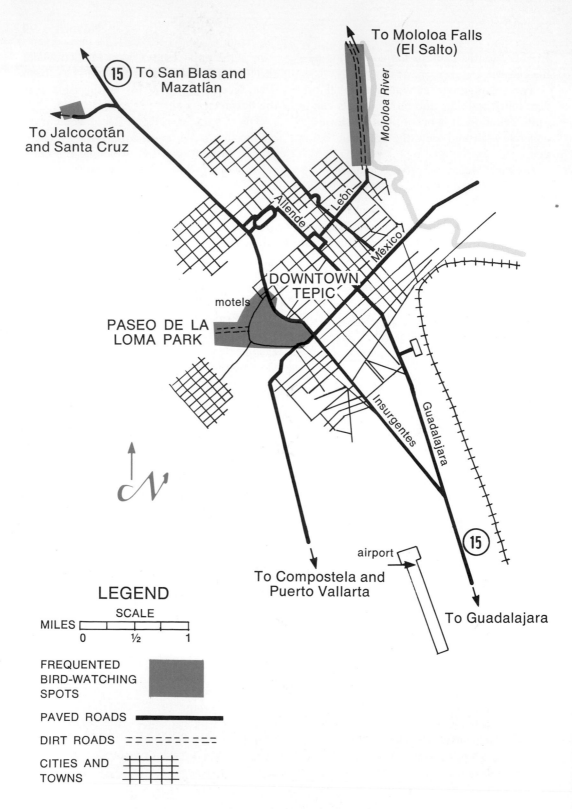

To Mololoa Falls
(El Salto)

Mololoa River

⑮ To San Blas and
Mazatlán

To Jalcocotán
and Santa Cruz

Allende

León

México

DOWNTOWN
TEPIC

motels

PASEO DE LA
LOMA PARK

Insurgentes

Guadalajara

N

To Compostela and
Puerto Vallarta

airport

⑮

To Guadalajara

LEGEND

SCALE
MILES

0   ½   1

FREQUENTED
BIRD-WATCHING
SPOTS

PAVED ROADS

DIRT ROADS

CITIES AND
TOWNS

TEPIC, NAYARIT

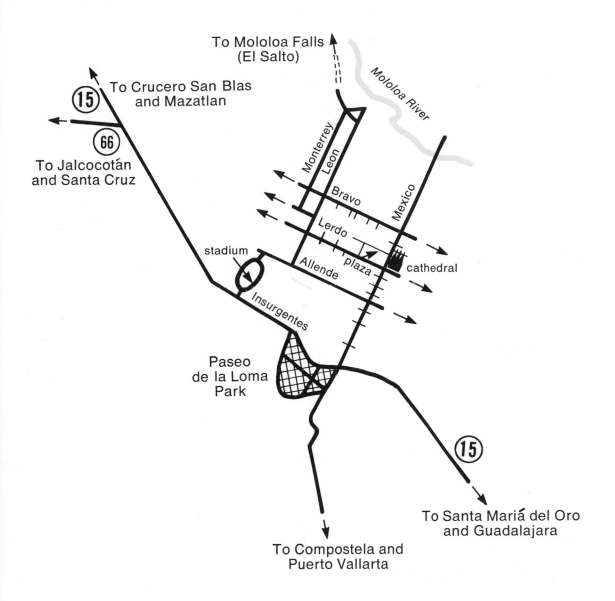

To Mololoa Falls
(El Salto)

Mololoa River

To Crucero San Blas
and Mazatlan

⑮

㊻

To Jalcocotán
and Santa Cruz

Monterrey

Leon

Bravo

Mexico

Lerdo

stadium

Allende

plaza

cathedral

Insurgentes

Paseo
de la Loma
Park

⑮

To Santa Mariá del Oro
and Guadalajara

To Compostela and
Puerto Vallarta

DOWNTOWN TEPIC, NAYARIT

TEPIC

As you enter Tepic you will see the pine-flanked slopes of Cerro San Juan rising in the west. The only sizable city between Mazatlán and Guadalajara, Tepic offers a number of fine accommodations, both downtown and along Highway 15.

A spacious, shady park called Paseo de la Loma is located along the highway. A walk through its north side and perhaps a stroll down a little cobblestone road that leads towards the mountain can provide pleasant hours of early morning bird watching.

Birds of Tepic I: Paseo De La Loma Park Area

Black Vulture   A
Inca Dove   A
Military Macaw   O   (*overhead*)
Blue-rumped Parrotlet   C
Groove-billed Ani   C
Plain-capped Star-throat   R
Broad-billed Hummingbird   C
Gila Woodpecker   A
Social Flycatcher   C
Kiskadee Flycatcher   C
Barn Swallow   A   (*migration*)
Purple Martin   C   (*migration*)
Mexican Crow   A
Rufous-backed Robin   A
Blue-Gray Gnatcatcher   A*
Ruby-crowned Kinglet   R*
Cedar Waxwing   R*
Solitary Vireo   O*
Warbling Vireo   O*
Orange-crowned Warbler   A*
Nashville Warbler   A*

Olive-backed Warbler   O
Audubon's Warbler   A*
Wilson's Warbler   C*
House Sparrow   A
Yellow-winged Cacique   A
Orchard Oriole   C
Hooded Oriole   C
Scarlet-headed Oriole   C
Baltimore Oriole   C   (*March and April*)
Bullock's Oriole   C*
Boat-tailed Grackle   A
Bronzed Cowbird   C
Western Tanager   C   (*migration*)
Yellow Grosbeak   O
Black-headed Grosbeak   C*
Blue Grosbeak   C
Indigo Bunting   A*
Lesser Goldfinch   A
Lark Sparrow   A*
Chipping Sparrow   A
Lincoln's Sparrow   A*

CERRO SAN JUAN

Take Highway 15 northwest out of town. After several miles, turn left (west) to follow Nayarit Route 66 as it winds over the lower slopes of Cerro San Juan.

Route 66 is little frequented, and you will find very few parking spots. One of them lies on the left about fourteen and one-half miles from the Highway 15 junction. A good trail heads uphill near a gravel bank here. A walk along it will give you a good glimpse of the interesting assortment of birds living together at this elevation of just under 4,000 feet. Long-needled Montezuma Pines grow next to species of tropical flora, and the bird life is similarly varied.

Birds of Tepic II: Cerro San Juan's Western Slopes

Turkey Vulture   A
Black Vulture   C

Red-tailed Hawk   C
Sparrow Hawk   C

White-winged Dove   C
Inca Dove   C
White-fronted Parrot   C
Lilac-crowned Parrot   O
Vaux's Swift   R*
Groove-billed Ani   C
Calliope Hummingbird   R   (*April migration*)
Berylline Hummingbird   C
Fork-tailed Emerald   O
Russet-crowned Motmot   C
Hairy Woodpecker   O
White-striped Woodcreeper   R
Thick-billed Kingbird   A
Social Flycatcher   A
Olivaceous Flycatcher   A
Western Flycatcher   A*
Tufted Flycatcher   C
Coues' Flycatcher   A*
Western Wood Pewee   R   (*migration*)
Rough-winged Swallow   C
Green Jay   R
Magpie-Jay   C
Bar-vented Wren   O
Happy Wren   O

Spotted Wren   C
Blue Mockingbird   C
Robin   R   (*April*)
White-throated Robin   C
Orange-billed Nightingale Thrush   C
Brown-backed Solitaire   A   (*loud, tumbling song*)
White-lored Gnatcatcher   O
Gray Silky Flycatcher   A   (*April*)
Townsend's Warbler   O*
Grace's Warbler   C
Black-throated Gray Warbler   O*
MacGillivray's Warbler   A*
Rufous-capped Warbler   O
Slate-throated Redstart   C
Hooded Oriole   C
Western Tanager   C*
Hepatic Tanager   C
Yellow Grosbeak   O
Black-headed Grosbeak   C*
Varied Bunting   A
Black-headed Siskin   C
Lesser Goldfinch   C
Rufous-sided Towhee   C
Lincoln's Sparrow   C*

ROUTE 66: JALCOCOTÁN TO SANTA CRUZ

ROUTE 66 DESCENDS from Cerro San Juan through increasingly tropical country. Banana trees cover the hills, and shady coffee fincas (ranches) fill the valleys. Nineteen miles from Tepic lies Jalcocotán, a major banana shipping point. Look for burro trains laden with bunches of bananas.

About a mile beyond Jalcocotán you will arrive at the small green roadside shrine that marks the junction of the rough Camino Real discussed on pages 95 through 98. If you haven't already done so, you may now want to take this jungle route which joins the Matanchen Bay road north to San Blas. In any event, look for the birds in the list on page 96, checking especially for Berylline

Hummingbirds and Rusty-crowned Ground Sparrows in the vicinity of the shrine.

As Route 66 continues west towards the sea the vegetation thins. Thick forests such as those of San Blas-Singaita and the Camino Real do not exist here. Only a few patches of tall trees grow in the ravines. Look for Squirrel Cuckoos, Coppery-tailed Trogons, Ivory-billed Woodcreepers, Rose-throated Becards, Masked Tityras, Pale-vented Euphonia and Yellow Grosbeaks.

Santa Cruz lies about twelve miles from Jalcocotán. It has no tourist facilities, although the projected new coastal highway from San Blas to Puerto Vallarta will probably change this situation. The nearby ocean shores are devoid of mangrove growth.

El Salto: Mololoa Falls

The Mololoa River cuts through the northern part of Tepic and can be crossed on either of two bridges. The waterfall (El Salto) of this river is an excellent place for bird watching.

To reach the falls from Tepic, follow the city's main north-south street, Avenida Mexico, north for two blocks beyond the plaza and cathedral. Turn left (west) onto Calle Bravo, drive about six blocks, then turn right (north) on either Calle León or Calle Monterrey. After four more blocks, turn left (west) onto the poor dirt road which leads to El Salto. About a mile or so beyond the edge of the city the road will fork; take the lefthand branch.

Numerous little ponds are located on both sides of the road to the falls. In the area around El Salto you will find field agriculture, dry hillsides, and many tall trees. Look for birds in all of these areas.

Birds of Tepic III: El Salto, the Mololoa Falls

Note: This locality has been visited only during early spring, and annual abundance symbols cannot be assigned at this writing.

Least Grebe	Bar-vented Wren
Green Heron	Long-billed Marsh Wren
Lesser Scaup	Rufous-backed Robin
Turkey Vulture	White-throated Robin
Jacana	Blue-Gray Gnatcatcher
Sora	White-lored Gnatcatcher
Common Gallinule	Water Pipit
American Coot	Bell's Vireo
Common Snipe	Orange-crowned Warbler
Spotted Sandpiper	Audubon's Warbler
Black-necked Stilt	Black-throated Gray Warbler
Mourning Dove	MacGillivray's Warbler
Inca Dove	Wilson's Warbler
Squirrel Cuckoo	Painted Redstart
Berylline Hummingbird	Yellow-winged Cacique
Cinnamon Hummingbird	Hooded Oriole
Fork-tailed Emerald	Scarlet-headed Oriole
Belted Kingfisher	Boat-tailed Grackle
Russet-crowned Motmot	Bronzed Cowbird
Ladder-backed Woodpecker	Blue Grosbeak
Gila Woodpecker	Varied Bunting
Cassin's Kingbird	Painted Bunting
Thick-billed Kingbird	White-collared Seedeater
Social Flycatcher	Lesser Goldfinch
Kiskadee Flycatcher	Rusty-crowned Ground Sparrow
Vermilion Flycatcher	Stripe-headed Sparrow
Black Phoebe	Grasshopper Sparrow
Magpie-Jay	Lark Sparrow
Blue Mockingbird	Lincoln's Sparrow

FINCHES

male

female

Ruddy-breasted Seedeater
Sporophila minuta

male

White-collared Seedeater
Sporophila torqueola

male

Blue Bunting
Cyanocompsa parellina

female

male

female

Blue-black Grassquit
Volatinia jacarina

Grayish Saltator
Saltator caerulescens

Yellow Grosbeak
Pheucticus chrysopeplus

Five-striped Sparrow
Aimophila quinquestriata

Rusty Sparrow
Aimophila rufescens

Rusty-crowned Ground Sparrow
Melozone kieneri

ROUTE 15: TEPIC TO THE JALISCO STATELINE

JALISCO IS a little more than sixty miles southeast of Tepic; Guadalajara is eighty-four miles from the Jalisco stateline. Several points of interest lie along this stretch of Route 15.

Ten miles outside of Tepic you will pass Cerro de Sanganguey, an extinct volcano that rises 7,716 feet. Santa Maria del Oro, a deep blue crater lake encircled by mountains, is a worthwhile side trip. The lake road branches to the right (east) twenty miles outside of Tepic. It winds through twelve miles of open country and wooded canyons before it reaches the water. The last several miles of the road has some good patches of tropical deciduous forest which host many birds. You may see some interesting species during strolls along the lake shore.

* * *

Route 15 continues southeast through dry pine and oak forests. Look for Berylline Hummingbirds, Tufted Flycatchers, Brown-backed Solitaires, Hepatic Tanagers, Black-headed Siskins, and other higher elevation species. As you continue towards Jalisco, you will pass dry agricultural habitats and a wide laval flow from Ceboruco, a volcano last active in 1870. Look for Stripe-headed Sparrows in the drier areas. Farther south, the road descends into a subtropical valley where stands of fruit trees host Blue-rumped Parrotlets, Groove-billed Anis, Rose-throated Becards, and Social Flycatchers.

The Nayarit-Jalisco border cuts across dry grassy hill country. If you continue south into Jalisco, you will traverse many steep barrancas. Just before you reach Magdelena, turn right on the first road beyond the railroad tracks. It will lead to a network of dirt roads around some large lagoons. Check this area for Western Grebes, egrets, Roseate Spoonbills, Fulvous Tree Ducks, and Jacanas.

Birds of Santa Maria Del Oro Lake

Eared Grebe   A
Least Grebe   C
Western Grebe   (*June record*)
Pied-billed Grebe   C
Olivaceous Cormorant   C
Sharp-shinned Hawk   C
Swainson's Hawk   A   (*migration*)
Rufous-bellied Chachalaca   C   (*noisy on some mornings*)
Blue-rumped Parrotlet   C
Squirrel Cuckoo   C
Ladder-backed Woodpecker   C
Pale-billed Woodpecker   C
Rose-throated Becard   C
Tropical Kingbird   A

Thick-billed Kingbird   C
Social Flycatcher   A
Kiskadee Flycatcher   A
Nutting's Flycatcher   A
Coues' Flycatcher   C
Western Wood Pewee   C   (*migration*)
Magpie-Jay   A
Mexican Crow   C
Yellow-Green Vireo   A   (*summer*)
Olive-backed Warbler   C
Yellow-winged Cacique   A
Scarlet-headed Oriole   A
Bronzed Cowbird   A
Lesser Goldfinch   A

Suggested Readings

Arizona Highways, XL (November, 1964). (Full issue on Sonora.)

Arellano, Marcos and Rojas, M. Paulino. *Aves Acuaticas Migratorias en Mexico.* Mexico D.F.: Instituto Mexicano de Recursos Naturales Renovables, A.C., 1956. (Good information on Mexican waterfowl, written in Spanish.)

Blake, E. R. *Birds of Mexico: Guide for Field Identification.* Chicago: University of Chicago Press, 1953. (The best general guide presently available.)

Cannon, Ray. *The Sea of Cortez.* Menlo Park, California: Lane Magazine and Book Company, 1966.

Edwards, Ernest P. *Finding Birds in Mexico.* Amherst, Virginia: Amherst Publishing Company, 1955. (Outdated and not comprehensive for west Mexico.)

Eisenmann, Eugene. *The Species of Middle American Birds.* ("Transactions of the Linnaean Society of New York," No. 7.) New York, 1955. (His names are widely accepted, follows fourth edition of *A.O.U. Checklist.*)

Ewing, R. C. (ed.). *Six Faces of Mexico.* Tucson: University of Arizona Press, 1966. (Excellent comprehensive work on Mexico.)

Friedmann, H., Griscom, Ludlow and Moore, R. T. *Distributional Checklist of the Birds of Mexico, Part I.* ("Pacific Coast Avifauna," No. 29.) Berkeley: Cooper Ornithological Club, 1950.

Gentry, Howard Scott. *Rio Mayo Plants.* ("Carnegie Institution of Washington Publications," No. 527.) Washington, D.C., 1952.

Grant, P. R. and Cowan, I. "A Review of the Avifuana of the Tres Marias Islands, Nayarit, Mexico." *Condor* Vol. 66 (May–June 1964), 221–228.

Gulick, Howard E. *Nayarit, Mexico, A Traveler's Guidebook.* Glendale, California: Arthur H. Clark Company, 1965. (A must if you go to Nayarit.)

Hilton, John W. *Sonora sketch book.* New York: The Macmillan Company, 1947. (Insight into Sonoran countryside and life.)

Leopold, A. Starker. *Wildlife of Mexico.* Berkeley and L.A.: University of California Press, 1959. (Contains useful information on all game birds and mammals.)

Miller, A. H., Friedman, H., Griscom, L. and Moore, R. T. *Distributional Checklist of the Birds of Mexico, Part II.* ("Pacific Coast Avifauna," No. 33.) Berkeley: Cooper Ornithological Society, 1957.

Pesman, M. Walter. *Flora Mexicana.* Globe, Arizona: Dale Stuart King, 1962.

Pfefferkorn, Ignaz. *Sonora, A Description of the Province.* Edited and Translated by Treutlein, Theodore. ("Coronado Historical Series," Vol. XII.) Albuquerque: University of New Mexico Press, 1949.

Peterson, Roger Tory. *A Field Guide to the Birds of Texas.* Boston: Houghton Mifflin Company, 1960.

Peterson, Roger Tory. *A Field Guide to Western Birds.* Boston: Houghton Mifflin Company, 1961.

Philips, Allan, Marshall, Joe and Monson, Gale. *The Birds of Arizona*. Tucson: University of Arizona Press, 1964.

Robbins, Chandler S., Bruun, Bertel and Zim, Herbert S. *A Guide to the Field Identification: Birds of North America*. New York: Golden Press, 1966. (New guide which treats all North American birds.)

Robertson, Thomas A., *A Southwestern Utopia*. Los Angeles: The Ward Ritchie Press, 1947. (Covers the Fuerte Valley, Sinaloa.)

Smithe, Frank B. *The Birds of Tikal*. Garden City, N.Y.: Natural History Press, 1966.

Stager, K. E. "The Avifuana of the Tres Marias Islands, Nayarit, Mexico." *Auk,* Vol. No. 74 (October, 1957), 413–432.

Sutton, George M., *Mexican Birds, First Impressions*. Norman: University of Oklahoma Press, 1951. (Useful chiefly in northeastern Mexico.)

Van Rossem, A. J., *A Distributional Survey of the Birds of Sonora, Mexico*. ("Occasional Papers of the Museum of Zoology of Louisiana State University," No. 21.) Baton Rouge: State University of Louisiana Press, 1945.

List of Bird Species

The following is a comprehensive list of all bird species which appear in this book. In general, the nomenclature follows that of the fifth edition of the *A.O.U. Checklist of North American Birds*. Nomenclature for species not found in the *Checklist* has been taken from *The Species of Middle American Birds* by Eugene Eisenmann.

There are 496 birds listed here, roughly one-half of the number known to occur in the entire country of Mexico.

TINAMOUS—*Tinamidae*
   Rufescent Tinamou (*Crypterellus cinnamomeus*)
LOONS—*Gaviidae*
   Common Loon (*Gavia immer*)
   Arctic Loon (*Gavia arctica*)
GREBES—*Podicipedidae*
   Eared Grebe (*Podiceps caspicus*)
   Least Grebe (*Podiceps dominicus*)
   Western Grebe (*Aechmophorus occidentalis*)
   Pied-billed Grebe (*Podilymbus podiceps*)
SHEARWATERS—*Procellariidae*
   Fulmar (*Fulmarus glacialis*)
   Pink-footed Shearwater (*Puffinus creatopus*)
   Sooty Shearwater (*Puffinus griseus*)
   Manx Shearwater (*Puffinus puffinus*)
STORM PETRELS—*Hydrobatidae*
   Black Petrel (*Oceanodroma melania*)
   Least Petrel (*Halocyptena microsoma*)
TROPICBIRDS—*Phaëthontidae*
   Red-billed Tropicbird (*Phaëthon aethereus*)
PELICANS—*Pelecanidae*
   White Pelican (*Pelecanus erythrorhynchos*)
   Brown Pelican (*Pelecanus occidentalis*)
BOOBIES—*Sulidae*
   Blue-footed Booby (*Sula nebouxii*)
   Brown Booby (*Sula leucogaster*)
CORMORANTS—*Phalacrocoracidae*
   Double-crested Cormorant (*Phalacrocorax auritus*)
   Olivaceous Cormorant (*Phalacrocorax olivaceus*)
   Brandt's Cormorant (*Phalacrocorax penicillatus*)
ANHINGAS—*Anhingidae*
   Anhinga (*Anhinga anhinga*)

109

FRIGATEBIRDS —*Fregatidae*
  Magnificent Frigatebird (*Fregata magnificens*)
HERONS AND BITTERNS—*Ardeidae*
  Great Blue Heron (*Ardea herodias*)
  Green Heron (*Butorides virescens*)
  Little Blue Heron (*Florida caerulea*)
  Cattle Egret (*Bubulcus ibis*)
  Reddish Egret (*Dichromanassa rufescens*)
  Common Egret (*Casmerodius albus*)
  Snowy Egret (*Leucophoyx thula*)
  Louisiana Heron (*Hydranassa tricolor*)
  Black-crowned Night Heron (*Nycticorax nycticorax*)
  Yellow-crowned Night Heron (*Nyctanassa violacea*)
  Bare-throated Tiger Heron (*Heterocnus mexicanus*)
  Least Bittern (*Ixobrychus exilis*)
  American Bittern (*Botaurus lentiginosus*)
BOAT-BILLED HERONS—*Cochleariidae*
  Boat-billed Heron (*Cochlearius cochlearius*)
STORKS AND WOOD IBIS—*Ciconiidae*
  Wood Ibis (*Mycteria americana*)
IBIS AND SPOONBILLS—*Threskiornithidae*
  White-faced Ibis (*Plegadis chihi*)
  White Ibis (*Eudocimus albus*)
  Roseate Spoonbill (*Ajaia ajaja*)
DUCKS AND GEESE—*Anatidae*
  White-fronted Goose (*Anser albifrons*)
  Snow Goose (*Chen hyperborea*)
  Black-bellied Tree Duck (*Dendrocygna autumnalis*)
  Fulvous Tree Duck (*Dendrocygna bicolor*)
  Muscovy (*Cairina moschata*)
  Mallard (*Anas platyrhynchos*)
  Gadwall (*Anas strepera*)
  Pintail (*Anas acuta*)
  Green-winged Teal (*Anas carolinensis*)
  Blue-winged Teal (*Anas discors*)
  Cinnamon Teal (*Anas cyanoptera*)
  American Widgeon (*Mareca americana*)
  Shoveler (*Spatula clypeata*)
  Redhead (*Aythya americana*)
  Ring-necked Duck (*Aythya collaris*)
  Canvasback (*Aythya valisineria*)
  Lesser Scaup (*Aythya affinis*)
  Common Goldeneye (*Bucephala clangula*)
  Bufflehead (*Bucephala albeola*)
  Surf Scoter (*Melanitta perspicillata*)
  Ruddy Duck (*Oxyura jamaicensis*)
  Common Merganser (*Mergus merganser*)
  Red-breasted Merganser (*Mergus serrator*)
NEW WORLD VULTURES—*Cathartidae*
  Turkey Vulture (*Cathartes aura*)
  Black Vulture (*Coragyps atratus*)
HAWKS, EAGLES, AND HARRIERS—*Accipitridae*
  Hook-billed Kite (*Chondrohierax uncinatus*)
  Sharp-shinned Hawk (*Accipiter striatus*)
  Cooper's Hawk (*Accipiter cooperii*)
  Red-tailed Hawk (*Buteo jamaicensis*)

Red-shouldered Hawk (*Buteo lineatus*)
Swainson's Hawk (*Buteo swainsoni*)
Zone-tailed Hawk (*Buteo albonotatus*)
Short-tailed Hawk (*Buteo brachyurus*)
White-tailed Hawk (*Buteo albicaudatus*)
Ferruginous Hawk (*Buteo regalis*)
Gray Hawk (*Buteo nitidus*)
Harris' Hawk (*Parabuteo unicinctus*)
Black-collared Hawk (*Busarellus nigricollis*)
Black Hawk (*Buteogallus anthracinus*)
Great Black Hawk (*Hypomorphnus urubitinga*)
Solitary Eagle (*Harpyhaliaetus solitarius*)
Golden Eagle (*Aquila chrysaetos*)
Marsh Hawk (*Circus cyaneus*)
Blackish Crane-Hawk (*Geranospiza nigra*)

OSPREY—*Pandionidae*
Osprey (*Pandion haliaetus*)

FALCONS—*Falconidae*
Laughing Falcon (*Herpetotheres cachinnans*)
Collared Forest-Falcon (*Micrastur semitorquatus*)
Caracara (*Caracara cheriway*)
Prairie Falcon (*Falco mexicanus*)
Peregrine Falcon (*Falco peregrinus*)
Bat Falcon (*Falco albigularis*)
Aplomado Falcon (*Falco femoralis*)
Pigeon Hawk (*Falco columbarius*)
Sparrow Hawk (*Falco sparverius*)

GUANS AND CHACHALACAS—*Cracidae*
Crested Guan (*Penelope purpurascens*)
Rufous-bellied Chachalaca (*Ortalis wagleri*)

QUAIL—*Phasianidae*
Gambel's Quail (*Lophortyx gambelii*)
Elegant Quail (*Lophortyx douglasii*)
Harlequin Quail (*Crytonyx montezumae*)

CRANES—*Gruidae*
Sandhill Crane (*Grus canadensis*)

RAILS, GALLINULES AND COOTS—*Rallidae*
Clapper Rail (*Rallus longirostris*)
Virginia Rail (*Rallus limicola*)
Rufous-necked Wood-Rail (*Aramides axillaris*)
Sora (*Porzana carolina*)
Purple Gallinule (*Porphyrula martinica*)
Common Gallinule (*Gallinula chloropus*)
American Coot (*Fulica americana*)

JACANAS—*Jacanidae*
Jacana (*Jacana spinosa*)

OYSTERCATCHERS—*Haematopodidae*
American Oystercatcher (*Haematopus palliatus*)

PLOVERS, TURNSTONES AND SURFBIRD—*Charadriidae*
Semipalmated Plover (*Charadrius semipalmatus*)
Snowy Plover (*Charadrius alexandrinus*)
Collared Plover (*Charadrius collaris*)
Wilson's Plover (*Charadrius wilsonia*)
Killdeer (*Charadrius vociferus*)
Mountain Plover (*Eupoda montana*)
Black-bellied Plover (*Squatarola squatarola*)

Surfbird (*Aphriza virgata*)
Ruddy Turnstone (*Arenaria interpres*)
Black Turnstone (*Arenaria melanocephala*)

SANDPIPERS—*Scolopacidae*
Common Snipe (*Capella gallinago*)
Long-billed Curlew (*Numenius americanus*)
Whimbrel (*Numenius phaeopus*)
Spotted Sandpiper (*Actitus macularia*)
Solitary Sandpiper (*Tringa solitaria*)
Wandering Tattler (*Heteroscelus incanus*)
Willet (*Catoptrophorus semipalmatus*)
Greater Yellowlegs (*Totanus melanoleucus*)
Lesser Yellowlegs (*Totanus flavipes*)
Knot (*Calidris canutus*)
Pectoral Sandpiper (*Erolia melanotos*)
Baird's Sandpiper (*Erolia bairdii*)
Least Sandpiper (*Erolia minutilla*)
Dunlin (*Erolia alpina*)
Short-billed Dowitcher (*Limnodromus griseus*)
Long-billed Dowitcher (*Limnodromus scolopaceus*)
Stilt Sandpiper (*Micropalama himantopus*)
Semipalmated Sandpiper (*Ereunetes pusillus*)
Western Sandpiper (*Ereunetes mauri*)
Marbled Godwit (*Limosa fedoa*)
Sanderling (*Crocethia alba*)

AVOCETS AND STILTS—*Recurvirostridae*
American Avocet (*Recurvirostra americana*)
Black-necked Stilt (*Himantopus mexicanus*)

PHALAROPES—*Phalaropodidae*
Red Phalarope (*Phalaropus fulicarius*)
Wilson's Phalarope (*Steganopus tricolor*)
Northern Phalarope (*Lobipes lobatus*)

JAEGERS—*Stercorariidae*
Pomarine Jaeger (*Stercorarius pomarinus*)
Parasitic Jaeger (*Stercorarius parasiticus*)

GULLS AND TERNS—*Laridae*
Glaucous-winged Gull (*Larus glaucescens*)
Western Gull (*Larus occidentalis*)
Herring Gull (*Larus argentatus*)
California Gull (*Larus californicus*)
Ring-billed Gull (*Larus delawarensis*)
Laughing Gull (*Larus atricilla*)
Franklin's Gull (*Larus pipixcan*)
Bonaparte's Gull (*Larus philadelphia*)
Heermann's Gull (*Larus heermanni*)
Sabine's Gull (*Xema sabini*)
Gull-billed Tern (*Gelochelidon nilotica*)
Forster's Tern (*Sterna forsteri*)
Common Tern (*Sterna hirundo*)
Sooty Tern (*Sterna fuscata*)
Least Tern (*Sterna albifrons*)
Royal Tern (*Thalasseus maximus*)
Elegant Tern (*Thalasseus elegans*)
Caspian Tern (*Hydroprogne caspia*)
Black Tern (*Chlidonias niger*)

SKIMMERS—*Rynchopidae*
  Black Skimmer (*Rynchops nigra*)

ALCIDS—*Alcidae*
  Xantus' Murrelet (*Endomychura hypoleuca*)

PIGEONS AND DOVES—*Columbidae*
  Band-tailed Pigeon (*Columba fasciata*)
  Red-billed Pigeon (*Columba flavirostris*)
  Rock Dove (*Columba livia*)
  White-winged Dove (*Zenaida asiatica*)
  Mourning Dove (*Zenaidura macroura*)
  Ground Dove (*Columbigallina passerina*)
  Ruddy Ground Dove (*Columbigallina talpacoti*)
  Inca Dove (*Scardafella inca*)
  White-fronted Dove (*Leptotila verreauxi*)
  Ruddy Quail Dove (*Geotrygon montana*)

PARROTS, PARAKEETS, AND MACAWS—*Psittaciformes*
  Military Macaw (*Ara militaris*)
  Green Parakeet (*Aratinga holochlora*)
  Orange-fronted Parakeet (*Aratinga canicularis*)
  Thick-billed Parrot (*Rhynchopsitta pachyrhyncha*)
  Blue-rumped Parrotlet (*Forpus cyanopygius*)
  White-fronted Parrot (*Amazona albifrons*)
  Lilac-crowned Parrot (*Amazona finschi*)

CUCKOOS, ROADRUNNERS, AND ANIS—*Cuculidae*
  Mangrove Cuckoo (*Coccyzus minor*)
  Yellow-billed Cuckoo (*Coccyzus americanus*)
  Squirrel Cuckoo (*Piaya cayana*)
  Lesser Ground Cuckoo (*Morococcyx erythropygus*)
  Roadrunner (*Geococcyx californianus*)
  Lesser Roadrunner (*Geococcyx velox*)
  Groove-billed Ani (*Crotophaga sulcirostris*)

BARN OWLS—*Tytonidae*
  Barn Owl (*Tyto alba*)

OWLS—*Strigidae*
  Whiskered Owl (*Otus trichopsis*)
  Flammulated Owl (*Otus flammeolus*)
  Great Horned Owl (*Bubo virginianus*)
  Least Pygmy Owl (*Glaucidium minutissimum*)
  Ferruginous Owl (*Glaucidium brasilianum*)
  Elf Owl (*Micrathene whitneyi*)
  Burrowing Owl (*Speotyto cunicularia*)
  Spotted Owl (*Strix occidentalis*)
  Mottled Owl (*Ciccaba virgata*)
  Long-eared Owl (*Asio otus*)
  Stygian Owl (*Asio stygius*)
  Short-eared Owl (*Asio flammeus*)

POTOOS—*Nyctibiidae*
  Common Potoo (*Nyctibius griseus*)

NIGHTJARS—*Caprimulgidae*
  Whip-poor-will (*Caprimulgus vociferus*)
  Buff-collared Nightjar (*Caprimulgus ridgwayi*)
  Pauraque (*Nyctidromus albicollis*)
  Common Nighthawk (*Chordeiles minor*)
  Lesser Nighthawk (*Chordeiles acutipennis*)

SWIFTS—*Apodidae*
 White-naped Swift (*Streptoprocne semicollaris*)
 Black Swift (*Cypseloides niger*)
 Vaux's Swift (*Chaetura vauxi*)
 White-throated Swift (*Aeronautes saxatalis*)
 Great Swallow-tailed Swift (*Panyptila sancti-hieronymi*)

HUMMINGBIRDS—*Trochilidae*
 Long-tailed Hermit (*Phaethornis superciliosus*)
 Lucifer Hummingbird (*Calothorax lucifer*)
 Black-chinned Hummingbird (*Archilochus alexandri*)
 Costa's Hummingbird (*Calypte costae*)
 Anna's Hummingbird (*Calypte anna*)
 Broad-tailed Hummingbird (*Selasphorus platycercus*)
 Rufous Hummingbird (*Selasphorus rufus*)
 Allen's Hummingbird (*Selasphorus sasin*)
 Heloise's Hummingbird (*Atthis heloisa*)
 Calliope Hummingbird (*Stellula calliope*)
 Plain-capped Star-throat (*Heliomaster constanti*)
 Blue-throated Hummingbird (*Lampornis clemenciae*)
 Rivoli's Hummingbird (*Eugenes fulgens*)
 Berylline Hummingbird (*Amazilia beryllina*)
 Cinnamon Hummingbird (*Amazilia rutila*)
 Violet-crowned Hummingbird (*Amazilia verticalis*)
 White-eared Hummingbird (*Hylocharis leucotis*)
 Fork-tailed Emerald (*Chlorostilbon canivetii*)
 Broad-billed Hummingbird (*Cynanthus latirostris*)

TROGONS—*Trogonidae*
 Eared Trogon (*Euptilotis neoxenus*)
 Citreoline Trogon (*Trogon citreolus*)
 Mountain Trogon (*Trogon mexicanus*)
 Coppery-tailed Trogon (*Trogon elegans*)

KINGFISHERS—*Alcedinidae*
 Belted Kingfisher (*Megaceryle alcyon*)
 Ringed Kingfisher (*Megaceryle torquata*)
 Amazon Kingfisher (*Chloroceryle amazona*)
 Green Kingfisher (*Chloroceryle americana*)

MOTMOTS—*Momotidae*
 Russet-crowned Motmot (*Momotus mexicanus*)

WOODPECKERS—*Picidae*
 Red-shafted Flicker (*Colaptes cafer*)
 Gilded Flicker (*Colaptes chrysoides*)
 Gray-crowned Woodpecker (*Piculus auricularis*)
 Linneated Woodpecker (*Dryocopus lineatus*)
 Gila Woodpecker (*Centurus uropygialus*)
 Golden-cheeked Woodpecker (*Centurus chrysogenys*)
 Acorn Woodpecker (*Melanerpes formicivorus*)
 Yellow-bellied Sapsucker (*Sphyrapicus varius*)
 Smoky-Brown Woodpecker (*Veniliornis fumigatus*)
 Hairy Woodpecker (*Dendrocopus villosus*)
 Ladder-backed Woodpecker (*Dendrocopus scalaris*)
 Arizona Woodpecker (*Dendrocopus arizonae*)
 Pale-billed Woodpecker (*Phloeoceastes guatemalensis*)

WOODCREEPERS—*Dendrocolaptidae*
 Ivory-billed Woodcreeper (*Xiphorhynchus flavigaster*)
 White-striped Woodcreeper (*Lepidocolaptes leucogaster*)

COTINGAS—*Cotingidae*
    Bright-rumped Attila (*Attila spadiceus*)
    Gray-collared Becard (*Pachyramphus major*)
    Rose-throated Becard (*Platypsaris aglaiae*)
    Masked Tityra (*Tityra semifasciata*)
TYRANT FLYCATCHERS—*Tyrannidae*
    Tropical Kingbird (*Tyrannus melancholicus*)
    Western Kingbird (*Tyrannus verticalis*)
    Cassin's Kingbird (*Tyrannus vociferans*)
    Thick-billed Kingbird (*Tyrannus crassirostris*)
    Scissor-tailed Flycatcher (*Muscivora forficata*)
    Boat-billed Flycatcher (*Megarynchus pitangua*)
    Social Flycatcher (*Myiozetetes similis*)
    Kiskadee Flycatcher (*Pitangus sulphuratus*)
    Sulphur-bellied Flycatcher (*Myiodynastes luteiventris*)
    Wied's Crested Flycatcher (*Myiarchus tyrannulus*)
    Ash-throated Flycatcher (*Myiarchus cinerascens*)
    Nutting's Flycatcher (*Myiarchus nuttingi*)
    Olivaceous Flycatcher (*Myiarchus tuberculifer*)
    Flammulated Flycatcher (*Deltarhynchus flammulatus*)
    Eastern Phoebe (*Sayornis phoebe*)
    Black Phoebe (*Sayornis nigricans*)
    Say's Phoebe (*Sayornis saya*)
    Traill's Flycatcher (*Empidonax traillii*)
    Hammond's Flycatcher (*Empidonax hammondii*)
    Dusky Flycatcher (*Empidonax oberholseri*)
    Gray Flycatcher (*Empidonax wrightii*)
    Pine Flycatcher (*Empidonax affinis*)
    Western Flycatcher (*Empidonax difficilis*)
    White-throated Flycatcher (*Empidonax albigularis*)
    Buff-breasted Flycatcher (*Empidonax fulvifrons*)
    Tufted Flycatcher (*Mitrephanes phaeocercus*)
    Coues' Flycatcher (*Contopus pertinax*)
    Western Wood Pewee (*Contopus sordidulus*)
    Olive-sided Flycatcher (*Nuttallornis borealis*)
    Vermilion Flycatcher (*Pyrocephalus rubinus*)
    Greenish Elaenia (*Myiopagis viridicata*)
    Beardless Flycatcher (*Camptosoma imberbe*)
SWALLOWS—*Hirundinidae*
    Violet-Green Swallow (*Tachycineta thalassina*)
    Tree Swallow (*Iridoprocne bicolor*)
    Mangrove Swallow (*Iridoprocne albilinea*)
    Bank Swallow (*Riparia riparia*)
    Rough-winged Swallow (*Stelgidopteryx ruficollis*)
    Barn Swallow (*Hirundo rustica*)
    Cliff Swallow (*Petrochelidon pyrrhonota*)
    Purple Martin (*Progne subis*)
    Gray-breasted Martin (*Progne chalybea*)
CORVIDS—*Corvidae*
    Steller's Jay (*Cyanocitta stelleri*)
    Mexican Jay (*Aphelocoma ultramarina*)
    Tufted Jay (*Cyanocorax dickeyi*)
    Green Jay (*Cyanocorax yncas*)
    San Blas Jay (*Cissilopha san-blasiana*)
    Purplish-backed Jay (*Cissilopha beecheii*)
    Magpie-Jay (*Calocitta formosa*)

Common Raven (*Corvus corax*)
White-necked Raven (*Corvus cryptoleucus*)
Mexican Crow (*Corvus imparatus*)
TITMICE—*Paridae*
Mexican Chickadee (*Parus sclateri*)
Bridled Titmouse (*Parus wollweberi*)
Verdin (*Auriparus flaviceps*)
Black-eared Bushtit (*Psaltriparus melanotis*)
NUTHATCHES—*Sittidae*
White-breasted Nuthatch (*Sitta carolinensis*)
CREEPERS—*Certhiidae*
Brown Creeper (*Certhiu familiaris*)
WRENS—*Troglodytidae*
House Wren (*Troglodytes aedon*)
Brown-throated Wren (*Troglodytes brunneicollis*)
Bewick's Wren (*Thryomanes bewickii*)
Bar-vented Wren (*Thryothorus sinaloa*)
Happy Wren (*Thryothorus felix*)
Cactus Wren (*Campylorhynchus brunneicapillus*)
Spotted Wren (*Campylorhynchus jocosus*)
Long-billed Marsh Wren (*Telmatodytes palustris*)
Canyon Wren (*Catherpes mexicanus*)
Rock Wren (*Salpinctes obsoletus*)
MIMICS—*Mimidae*
Mockingbird (*Mimus polyglottos*)
Blue Mockingbird (*Melanotis caerulescens*)
Bendire's Thrasher (*Toxostoma bendirei*)
Curve-billed Thrasher (*Toxostoma curvirostre*)
Le Conte's Thrasher (*Toxostoma lecontei*)
Crissal Thrasher (*Toxostoma dorsale*)
Sage Thrasher (*Oreoscoptes montanus*)
THRUSHES—*Turdidae*
Robin (*Turdus migratorius*)
Rufous-backed Robin (*Turdus rufo-palliatus*)
White-throated Robin (*Turdus assimilis*)
Wood Thrush (*Hylocichla mustelina*)
Hermit Thrush (*Hylocichla guttata*)
Swainson's Thrush (*Hylocichla ustulata*)
Russet Nightingale-Thrush (*Catharus occidentalis*)
Orange-billed Nightingale-Thrush (*Catharus aurantiirostris*)
Eastern Bluebird (*Sialia sialis*)
Western Bluebird (*Sialia mexicana*)
Mountain Bluebird (*Sialia currucoides*)
Brown-backed Solitaire (*Myadestes obscurus*)
GNATCATCHERS AND KINGLETS—*Sylviidae*
Blue-Gray Gnatcatcher (*Polioptila caerulea*)
White-lored Gnatcatcher (*Polioptila albiloris*)
Black-capped Gnatcatcher (*Polioptila nigriceps*)
Black-tailed Gnatcatcher (*Polioptila melanura*)
Golden-crowned Kinglet (*Regulus satrapa*)
Ruby-crowned Kinglet (*Regulus calendula*)
PIPITS—*Motacillidae*
Water Pipit (*Anthus spinoletta*)
WAXWINGS—*Bombycillidae*
Cedar Waxwing (*Bombycilla cedrorum*)

SILKY FLYCATCHERS—*Ptilogonatidae*
    Gray Silky Flycatcher (*Ptilogonys cinereus*)
    Phainopepla (*Phainopepla nitens*)

SHRIKES—*Laniidae*
    Loggerhead Shrike (*Lanius ludovicianus*)

STARLINGS—*Sturnidae*
    Starling (*Sturnus vulgaris*)

VIREOS—*Vireonidae*
    Black-capped Vireo (*Vireo atricapilla*)
    Mangrove Vireo (*Vireo pallens*)
    Hutton's Vireo (*Vireo huttoni*)
    Golden Vireo (*Vireo hypochryseus*)
    Bell's Vireo (*Vireo bellii*)
    Gray Vireo (*Vireo vicinior*)
    Yellow-throated Vireo (*Vireo flavifrons*)
    Solitary Vireo (*Vireo solitarius*)
    Yellow-Green Vireo (*Vireo flavoviridis*)
    Philadelphia Vireo (*Vireo philadelphicus*)
    Warbling Vireo (*Vireo gilvus*)

WOOD WARBLERS—*Parulidae*
    Black-and-White Warbler (*Mniotilta varia*)
    Worm-eating Warbler (*Helmitheros vermivorus*)
    Tennessee Warbler (*Vermivora peregrina*)
    Orange-crowned Warbler (*Vermivora celata*)
    Nashville Warbler (*Vermivora ruficapilla*)
    Virginia's Warbler (*Vermivora virginiae*)
    Lucy's Warbler (*Vermivora luciae*)
    Crescent-chested Warbler (*Vermivora superciliosa*)
    Olive-backed Warbler (*Parula pitiayumi*)
    Yellow Warbler (*Dendroica petechia*)
    Audubon's Warbler (*Dendroica auduboni*)
    Black-throated Gray Warbler (*Dendroica nigrescens*)
    Townsend's Warbler (*Dendroica townsendi*)
    Black-throated Green Warbler (*Dendroica virens*)
    Hermit Warbler (*Dendroica occidentalis*)
    Yellow-throated Warbler (*Dendroica dominica*)
    Grace's Warbler (*Dendroica graciae*)
    Chesnut-sided Warbler (*Dendroica pensylvanica*)
    Palm Warbler (*Dendroica palmarum*)
    Ovenbird (*Seiurus aurocapillus*)
    Northern Waterthrush (*Seiurus noveboracensis*)
    Louisiana Waterthrush (*Seiurus motacilla*)
    Kentucky Warbler (*Oporornis formosus*)
    MacGillivray's Warbler (*Oporornis tolmiei*)
    Yellowthroat (*Geothlypis trichas*)
    Ground Chat (*Chamaethylypis poliocephala*)
    Yellow-breasted Chat (*Icteria virens*)
    Red-breasted Chat (*Granatellus venustus*)
    Fan-tailed Warbler (*Euthlypis lachrymosa*)
    Red Warbler (*Ergaticus ruber*)
    Golden-browed Warbler (*Basileuterus belli*)
    Rufous-capped Warbler (*Basileuterus rufifrons*)
    Red-faced Warbler (*Cardellina rubrifrons*)
    Hooded Warbler (*Wilsonia citrina*)
    Wilson's Warbler (*Wilsonia pusilla*)
    American Redstart (*Setophaga ruticilla*)

Painted Redstart (*Setophaga picta*)
Slate-throated Redstart (*Myioborus miniatus*)

WEAVER FINCHES—*Ploceidae*
House Sparrow (*Passer domesticus*)

ICTERIDS—*Icteridae*
Yellow-winged Cacique (*Cassiculus melanicterus*)
Eastern Meadowlark (*Sturnella magna*)
Western Meadowlark (*Sturnella neglecta*)
Yellow-headed Blackbird (*Xanthocephalus xanthocephalus*)
Red-winged Blackbird (*Agelaius phoeniceus*)
Orchard Oriole (*Icterus spurius*)
Hooded Oriole (*Icterus cucullatus*)
Scarlet-headed Oriole (*Icterus pustulatus*)
Black-vented Oriole (*Icterus wagleri*)
Scott's Oriole (*Icterus parisorum*)
Baltimore Oriole (*Icterus galbula*)
Bullock's Oriole (*Icterus bullockii*)
Brewer's Blackbird (*Euphagus cyanocephalus*)
Boat-tailed Grackle (*Cassidix mexicanus*)
Brown-headed Cowbird (*Molothrus ater*)
Bronzed Cowbird (*Tangavius aeneus*)

TANAGERS—*Thraupidae*
Blue-hooded Euphonia (*Tanagra elegantissima*)
Pale-vented Euphonia (*Tanagra godmani*)
Western Tanager (*Piranga ludoviciana*)
Scarlet Tanager (*Piranga olivacea*)
Hepatic Tanager (*Piranga flava*)
Summer Tanager (*Piranga rubra*)
Flame-colored Tanager (*Piranga bidentata*)
Red-headed Tanager (*Piranga erythrocephala*)
Red-crowned Ant-Tanager (*Habia rubica*)
Rose-breasted Thrush-Tanager (*Rhodinocichla rosea*)

FINCHES—*Fringillidae*
Grayish Saltator (*Saltator coerulescens*)
Cardinal (*Richmondena cardinalis*)
Pyrrhuloxia (*Pyrrhuloxia sinuata*)
Yellow Grosbeak (*Pheucticus chrysopeplus*)
Rose-breasted Grosbeak (*Pheucticus ludovicianus*)
Black-headed Grosbeak (*Pheucticus melanocephalus*)
Blue Grosbeak (*Guiraca caerulea*)
Blue Bunting (*Cyanocompsa parellina*)
Indigo Bunting (*Passerina cyanea*)
Lazuli Bunting (*Passerina amoena*)
Varied Bunting (*Passerina versicolor*)
Painted Bunting (*Passerina ciris*)
Dickcissel (*Spiza americana*)
Hooded Grosbeak (*Hesperiphona abeillei*)
Purple Finch (*Carpodacus purpureus*)
House Finch (*Carpodacus mexicanus*)
White-collared Seedeater (*Sporophila torqueola*)
Ruddy-breasted Seedeater (*Sporophila minuta*)
Blue-Black Grassquit (*Volatinia jacarina*)
Pine Siskin (*Spinus pinus*)
Black-headed Siskin (*Spinus notatus*)
American Goldfinch (*Spinus tristis*)
Lesser Goldfinch (*Spinus psaltria*)

Lawrence's Goldfinch (*Spinus lawrencei*)
Rufous-capped Brush-Finch (*Atlapetes pileatus*)
Green-striped Brush-Finch (*Atlapetes virenticeps*)
Olive Sparrow (*Arremonops rufivirgata*)
Green-tailed Towhee (*Chlorura chlorura*)
Rufous-sided Towhee (*Pipilo erythrophthalmus*)
Brown Towhee (*Pipilo fuscus*)
Rusty-crowned Ground Sparrow (*Melozone kieneri*)
Striped Sparrow (*Oriturus Superciliosus*)
Lark Bunting (*Calamospiza melonocorys*)
Savannah Sparrow (*Passerculus sandwichensis*)
Grasshopper Sparrow (*Ammodramus savannarum*)
Vesper Sparrow (*Pooecetes gramineus*)
Lark Sparrow (*Chondestes grammacus*)
Five-striped Sparrow (*Aimophila quinquestriata*)
Stripe-headed Sparrow (*Aimophila ruficauda*)
Rufous-winged Sparrow (*Aimophila carpalis*)
Rusty Sparrow (*Aimophila rufescens*)
Rufous-crowned Sparrow (*Aimophila ruficeps*)
Botteri's Sparrow (*Aimophila botterii*)
Cassin's Sparrow (*Aimophila cassinii*)
Black-throated Sparrow (*Amphispiza bilineata*)
Sage Sparrow (*Amphispiza belli*)
Gray-headed Junco (*Junco caniceps*)
Mexican Junco (*Junco phaeonotus*)
Chipping Sparrow (*Spizella passerina*)
Clay-colored Sparrow (*Spizella pallida*)
Brewer's Sparrow (*Spizella breweri*)
White-crowned Sparrow (*Zonotrichia leucophrys*)
Golden-crowned Sparrow (*Zonotrichia atricapilla*)
White-throated Sparrow (*Zonotrichia albicollis*)
Lincoln's Sparrow (*Melospiza lincolnii*)
Swamp Sparrow (*Melospiza georgiana*)
Song Sparrow (*Melospiza melodia*)

Christmas Bird Counts at San Blas, Nayarit 1964, 1965, 1966, 1967

For four years the author has been organizing groups to take Christmas bird counts in the area around San Blas, Nayarit, modeled after the familiar counts sponsored by the National Audubon Society all over the United States and Canada.

The area covered by the count lies within a fifteen mile diameter circle centered six and one half miles due east of the zocolo in San Blas. Most of the areas covered in the text are included in this circle: the heavy tropical San Blas-Singaita jungle, the watery seasonal lagoons, the mangrove swamps of the Estero San Cristóbal and other estuaries, the booby rock, the coastal habitats of Matanchen Bay, the plantations along the old Camino Real, the town of San Blas, and habitats along the trails.

Many of the areas within the circle are beyond the reach of boats and vehicles at this time. We have only counted birds in the generally accessible areas and do not pretend to have counted every bird and correctly identified every species. Only by long continuation of the Christmas count can we eventually hope to procure useful statistics on the birds in this rich bird watching area.

The four years of counts which follow can serve several purposes. From them you can glean information on the trends in bird distribution and population as it occurs in the San Blas area. You also might infer an estimate of the efficiency of the amateur bird watcher in a tropical environment. If, of course, you are interested in joining the counting group some Christmas, the tradition can provide you with some really self-disciplined sport. Each of the counts take four days to procure, including Christmas day. Write to me in care of the University of Arizona Press if you are interested in joining the Christmas count group.

YEAR	Number of Species	Number of Individual Birds	Number of Bird-watchers
1964	210	13,225	6
1965	210	21,876	19
1966	209	19,111	27
1967	220	26,690	21

CHRISTMAS COUNTS AT SAN BLAS, NAYARIT

YEAR	1964	1965	1966	1967
Eared Grebe	0	0	1	1
Least Grebe	6	1	12	5
Pied-billed Grebe	1	1	8	7
White Pelican	34	55	21	55
Brown Pelican	807	405	634	358
Blue-footed Booby	32	0	137	2
Brown Booby	52	2	1	0
Double-crested Cormorant	0	5	3	0
Olivaceous Cormorant	242	408	162	202
Anhinga	55	81	82	50
Magnificent Frigatebird	170	84	331	292
Great Blue Heron	17	18	17	55
Green Heron	40	58	82	95
Little Blue Heron	27	55	64	187
Cattle Egret	27	0	14	7
Reddish Egret	4	1	3	1
Common Egret	70	281	324	655
Snowy Egret	137	439	224	1102
Louisiana Heron	24	61	24	262
Black-crowned Night Heron	75	88	31	40
Yellow-crowned Night Heron	50	20	68	67
Bare-throated Tiger Heron	12	6	3	2
Least Bittern	1	0	0	0
Boat-billed Heron	60	65	55	72
Wood Ibis	117	163	128	48
White-faced Ibis	1	129	50	34
White Ibis	135	319	383	376
Roseate Spoonbill	36	66	19	42
Black-bellied Tree Duck	80	335	26	8
Muscovy Duck	0	4	0	6
Gadwall	2	186	31	510
Pintail	25	290	104	900
Green-winged Teal	713	2660	462	1250
Blue-winged Teal	44	87	173	925
Cinnamon Teal	50	395	270	410
American Widgeon	25	42	174	490
Shoveler	85	336	219	1100
Ring-necked Duck	0	0	6	0
Lesser Scaup	408	1	81	80
Surf Scoter	0	13	0	0
Ruddy Duck	0	0	0	3
Turkey Vulture	110	158	226	332
Black Vulture	170	213	263	137
Sharp-shinned Hawk	1	0	0	1
Cooper's Hawk	1	1	0	0
Red-tailed Hawk	1	2	2	0
Zone-tailed Hawk	1	0	5	1
Short-tailed Hawk	0	1	5	5
White-tailed Hawk	0	1	0	1
Gray Hawk	6	5	4	7
Harris' Hawk	4	3	2	4
Black Hawk	4	11	5	4
Great Black Hawk	3	0	1	0
Marsh Hawk	3	2	0	1

YEAR	1964	1965	1966	1967
Blackish Crane-Hawk	0	1	1	0
Osprey	5	7	6	6
Laughing Falcon	1	1	1	0
Collared Forest-Falcon	1	0	0	0
Caracara	9	5	8	10
Peregrine Falcon	0	0	0	1
Sparrow Hawk	3	8	10	5
Rufous-bellied Chachalaca	0	5	0	8
Elegant Quail	0	7	5	9
Clapper Rail	1	0	2	0
Rufous-necked Wood-Rail	0	0	1	0
Sora	1	10	8	10
Common Gallinule	87	126	68	78
American Coot	110	442	384	1500
Jacana	43	35	63	17
American Oystercatcher	0	4	2	0
Semipalmated Plover	40	61	33	25
Snowy Plover	0	2	14	3
Collared Plover	1	0	0	0
Wilson's Plover	7	236	842	22
Killdeer	15	2	37	11
Black-bellied Plover	18	17	122	16
Surfbird	12	0	0	0
Ruddy Turnstone	40	11	6	8
Common Snipe	2	1	0	4
Long-billed Curlew	7	14	25	5
Whimbrel	12	26	32	14
Spotted Sandpiper	24	18	44	36
Solitary Sandpiper	1	2	0	2
Wandering Tattler	20	0	7	0
Willet	466	199	141	68
Greater Yellowlegs	21	281	230	450
Lesser Yellowlegs	127	375	237	600
Knot	30	6	14	40
Least Sandpiper	32	393	536	1306
Dunlin	5	1	18	0
Dowitcher, species	1080	933	592	1300
Stilt Sandpiper	2	141	66	760
Semipalmated Sandpiper	0	0	0	300
Western Sandpiper	410	740	615	850
Marbled Godwit	39	52	34	8
Sanderling	1100	946	815	330
American-Avocet	400	735	430	630
Black-necked Stilt	153	631	386	904
Wilson's Phalarope	0	0	0	1
Glaucous-winged Gull	1	0	0	0
Western Gull	0	1	0	0
Herring Gull	1	5	0	0
California Gull	0	6	1	0
Ring-billed Gull	5	18	7	4
Laughing Gull	6	10	0	0
Bonaparte's Gull	1	0	1	1
Heermann's Gull	71	34	10	2
Gull-billed Tern	5	2	9	6
Forster's Tern	25	2	25	22

YEAR	1964	1965	1966	1967
Common Tern	26	9	1	8
Royal Tern	1	17	1	2
Elegant Tern	1	7	3	3
Caspian Tern	22	8	27	44
Black Skimmer	160	175	350	55
Red-billed Pigeon	6	2	19	6
White-winged Dove	1500	1391	1946	1477
Mourning Dove	1	0	1	2
Ground Dove	79	21	136	51
Ruddy Ground Dove	28	28	21	80
Inca Dove	1	0	1	1
White-fronted Dove	17	2	12	5
Ruddy Quail Dove	3	1	1	0
Military Macaw	16	38	0	0
Orange-fronted Parakeet	132	252	422	629
Blue-rumped Parrotlet	90	174	80	228
White-fronted Parrot	271	139	136	226
Lilac-crowned Parrot	4	52	40	22
Mangrove Cuckoo	0	1	0	0
Squirrel Cuckoo	3	2	3	4
Lesser Roadrunner	0	1	0	0
Groove-billed Ani	57	56	201	165
Ferruginous Owl	1	1	1	2
Mottled Owl	1	0	0	0
Common Potoo	5	9	2	12
Pauraque	3	7	3	8
Lesser Nighthawk	4	27	0	112
Vaux's Swift	33	269	61	267
Long-tailed Hermit	5	4	4	2
Black-chinned Hummingbird	0	0	1	4
Plain-capped Star-throat	1	2	2	1
Berylline Hummingbird	3	4	3	2
Cinnamon Hummingbird	39	51	45	43
Violet-crowned Hummingbird	0	7	6	1
Fork-tailed Emerald	4	8	3	4
Broad-billed Hummingbird	5	22	35	5
Citreoline Trogon	6	8	18	5
Coppery-tailed Trogon	2	3	6	2
Belted Kingfisher	19	12	22	27
Ringed Kingfisher	0	2	3	2
Green Kingfisher	28	25	27	26
Russet-crowned Motmot	2	5	4	6
Gray-crowned Woodpecker	0	0	2	0
Linneated Woodpecker	4	11	16	8
Golden-cheeked Woodpecker	53	75	79	92
Ladder-backed Woodpecker	0	0	1	0
Pale-billed Woodpecker	5	5	3	12
Ivory-billed Woodcreeper	2	9	7	5
Rose-throated Becard	10	4	9	11
Masked Tityra	14	20	31	16
Tropical Kingbird	111	110	92	146
Thick-billed Kingbird	7	32	24	60
Boat-billed Flycatcher	4	0	2	5
Social Flycatcher	29	87	92	109
Kiskadee Flycatcher	20	55	68	75

YEAR	1964	1965	1966	1967
Myiarchus, large size (Wied's and/or Great Crested)	2	1	1	2
Myiarchus, medium size (Nutting's and/or Ash-throated)	2	4	3	2
Olivaceous Flycatcher	24	19	10	9
Flammulated Flycatcher	0	0	0	1
Empidonax, light-breasted (White-throated, Dusky, Least, and/or Others)	9	13	3	5
Empidonax, yellow-breasted (Western and/or Yellow-bellied)	11	9	17	14
Tufted Flycatcher	2	0	0	2
Coues' Flycatcher	3	18	6	3
Wood Pewee, species (Western and/or Eastern)	0	1	1	0
Vermilion Flycatcher	12	23	29	26
Greenish Elaenia	1	0	0	1
Beardless Flycatcher	0	1	2	0
Bank Swallow	0	0	0	2
Mangrove Swallow	145	110	204	420
Rough-winged Swallow	454	149	448	573
Gray-breasted Martin	40	112	141	225
Green Jay	0	0	0	3
San Blas Jay	2	5	3	0
Magpie-Jay	8	12	11	8
Common Raven	0	1	0	2
Mexican Crow	113	251	346	543
House Wren	0	2	2	1
Bar-vented Wren	23	5	16	17
Happy Wren	23	23	26	38
Long-billed Marsh Wren	0	0	1	0
Mockingbird	4	4	17	2
Blue Mockingbird	8	16	13	11
Rufous-backed Robin	49	67	29	37
White-throated Robin	1	26	1	24
Swainson's Thrush	0	2	0	1
Orange-billed Nightingale-Thrush	0	1	0	2
Blue-Gray Gnatcatcher	46	65	58	78
White-lored Gnatcatcher	1	0	0	1
Ruby-crowned Kinglet	1	0	0	1
Water Pipit	3	8	5	2
Black-capped Vireo	6	4	4	1
Mangrove Vireo	1	0	0	0
Golden Vireo	1	1	0	2
Bell's Vireo	1	2	0	2
Solitary Vireo	2	0	3	5
Philadelphia Vireo	1	0	0	0
Warbling Vireo	4	17	5	20
Black-and-White Warbler	2	0	2	3
Orange-crowned Warbler	20	35	17	14
Nashville Warbler	48	38	33	54
Virginia's Warbler	0	0	0	1
Olive-backed Warbler	19	15	24	17
Yellow Warbler	67	56	71	72
Audubon's Warbler	35	65	18	50

YEAR	1964	1965	1966	1967
Black-throated Gray Warbler	11	20	28	14
Black-throated Green Warbler	0	0	0	1
Chesnut-sided Warbler	0	0	0	1
Palm Warbler	1	0	0	0
Northern Waterthrush	9	4	13	41
Louisiana Waterthrush	1	0	0	0
MacGillivray's Warbler	30	17	17	13
Yellowthroat	2	2	7	14
Ground Chat	3	0	1	1
Yellow-breasted Chat	5	6	8	8
Red-breasted Chat	0	1	0	0
Fan-tailed Warbler	0	1	0	0
Wilson's Warbler	53	58	22	87
American Redstart	38	40	81	62
House Sparrow	17	24	29	20
Yellow-winged Cacique	415	368	664	183
Red-winged Blackbird	0	80	41	30
Orchard Oriole	1	18	9	44
Hooded Oriole	10	14	9	8
Scarlet-headed Oriole	33	45	67	51
Black-vented Oriole	0	2	1	0
Baltimore Oriole	0	0	0	3
Bullock's Oriole	1	2	1	1
Boat-tailed Grackle	265	1121	904	565
Bronzed Cowbird	30	340	615	285
Pale-vented Euphonia	0	6	5	10
Western Tanager	1	0	0	4
Summer Tanager	2	7	19	6
Red-crowned Ant-Tanager	19	2	8	26
Grayish Saltator	20	64	38	34
Yellow Grosbeak	1	10	3	1
Rose-breasted Grosbeak	0	2	0	1
Black-headed Grosbeak	7	4	1	11
Blue Grosbeak	2	5	7	38
Blue Bunting	0	0	3	1
Indigo Bunting	2	0	2	5
Varied Bunting	13	9	5	17
Painted Bunting	20	18	28	36
Dickcissel	0	14	0	1
House Finch	0	0	1	0
White-collared Seedeater	12	11	65	91
Ruddy-breasted Seedeater	2	0	0	0
Blue-Black Grassquit	0	1	17	5
Lesser Goldfinch	0	6	5	0
Green-tailed Towhee	0	1	0	1
Rusty-crowned Ground Sparrow	0	1	2	2
Savannah Sparrow	3	0	2	4
Vesper Sparrow	0	0	0	3
Lark Sparrow	1	0	4	2
Stripe-headed Sparrow	2	4	0	10
Lincoln's Sparrow	9	8	10	5

INDEX

PLACE NAMES

BIRDS

NOTES

NOTES

NOTES

NOTES

NOTES

NOTES